Red River Girl

Norma Sommerdorf

Holiday House / New York

The epigraph on p. v is from *Floral Home, or, First Years of Minnesota* by Harriet Bishop, N
York: Sheldon Blakeman and Company, 1857.

Library of Congress Cataloging-in-Publication Data
Sommerdorf, Norma.
Red River girl / by Norma Sommerdorf.—1st ed.
p.   cm.
Summary: In a diary covering the years 1846 to 1848, a young Metis
teenager describes her journey from St. Eustace, Québec, to St. Paul,
Minnesota, where she settles with her family and decides to become
a teacher.
ISBN-13: 978-0-8234-1903-6 (hardcover)
ISBN-10: 0-8234-1903-7 (hardcover)
[1. Frontier and pioneer life—Fiction. 2. Metis—Fiction. 3. Teachers
—Fiction. 4. Saint Paul (Minn.)—History—19th century—Fiction.
5. Red River of the North—Fiction. 6. Diaries—Fiction.] I. Title.
PZ7.S6968Red 2006
[Fic]—dc22   2006002017

To those who teach
and make the world a better place
for everyone

July 25, 1847

St. Paul, Minnesota

"There were seven scholars that day—
three white children and four half-breeds,
and one visitor, a half-breed woman.
It was necessary to have an interpreter.
A large half-breed girl was found
who could speak English, French and Sioux."

Harriet Bishop,
First Public School Teacher
in Minnesota

WHO WAS THAT GIRL?

Contents

Foreword

French explorers arrived in eastern Canada more than three hundred years before this story begins. In 1535 Jacques Cartier discovered the eastern shore of Canada and the St. Lawrence River, which connects the Great Lakes to the Atlantic Ocean. In 1609 Samuel de Champlain brought with him a group of forty settlers. Europeans wanted furs, especially beaver, to make hats that wealthy men wore, and Champlain sent out traders to buy furs from the Native Americans. This was the beginning of what became the fur trade.

Voyageurs, who were often French men, brought the furs east by canoe from the wooded inland of the North American continent, for shipping to Europe. Native Americans trapped the animals and exchanged the pelts for kettles, axes, beads, and other goods at trading posts.

By the 1840s many people in the Red River Settlement (Winnipeg and St. Boniface, Manitoba) were descendants of voyageurs and their Indian wives. They spoke French but practiced Native American patterns of living. These people were known as Métis (MAY-tee), a French word meaning "mixed blood."

The girl who helped Harriet Bishop was most likely Métis, but no other mention can be found of her in historical documents. In the story that follows, Josette, her father, brothers, relatives, and the families she came to know on her travels are fictitious.

Acknowledgments

The wealth of resources at the Minnesota Historical Society Library provided the base of research for this book, and led to visits to the Pembina Museum, Pembina, ND; Kittson County Museum, Lake Bronson, MN; and St. Boniface Museum and St. Norbert Provincial Heritage Park, both near Winnipeg, Manitoba. Visits to Galena, IL, and St. Louis, MO, also supplied background.

Young adult readers who were encouraging after reading an early manuscript were Megan Cahill, Colleen Cahill, and Kelly Dockendorf. Writers groups who gave helpful suggestions include Arvella Whitmore's group, especially Joanne Reisberg; and the East Wing Writers Group: Heidi Grosch, Joan Linck, Lissa Johnston, and Julie Schuster.

Thanks are due Ojibwe friends who shared their knowledge and traditions: Loretta Porter Knutson, Orr, MN; Gene Begay, St. Paul, MN; and William Annis, interpreter at the Folle Avoinne Historical Park, Danbury, WI. Many thanks also to Jacques Deseve, Danbury, WI, whose loan of copies of *The Beaver Magazine* included a profile of the Nolin sisters. Thanks, too, to Málina Brown Mangal, who supplied French translation when needed. And special thanks to my husband for his continuing patience and support.

I am also grateful for a grant from the Minnesota State Arts Board, which makes possible visits to schools and libraries in communities along the Red River Trail and other parts of the state.

Finally, thanks to my counselor and agent, Barbara Markowitz, and to my editor, Mary Cash, whose experience and interest in the subject added to the editing process.

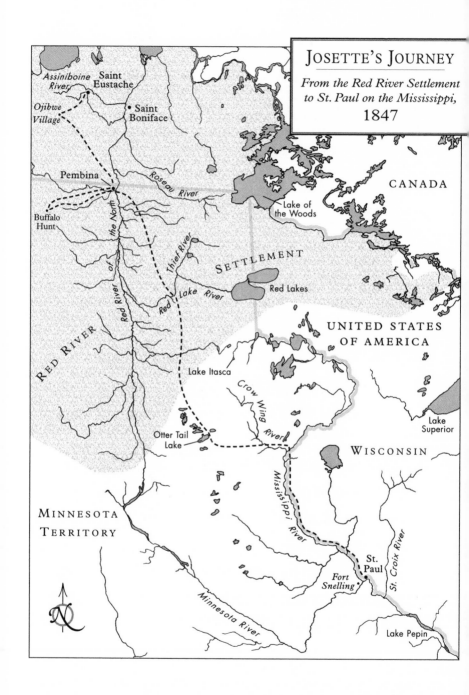

JOSETTE'S JOURNEY

From the Red River Settlement to St. Paul on the Mississippi,
1847

Assiniboine River
Saint Eustache
Ojibwe Village
Saint Boniface
Pembina
Roseau River
CANADA
Lake of the Woods
Buffalo Hunt
Red River of the North
Thief River
Red Lake River
SETTLEMENT
Red Lakes
UNITED STATES OF AMERICA
RED RIVER
Lake Itasca
Crow Wing River
Lake Superior
Otter Tail Lake
WISCONSIN
MINNESOTA TERRITORY
Mississippi River
St. Paul
Fort Snelling
St. Croix River
Minnesota River
Lake Pepin

1. My Life in the Red River Settlement

Tuesday, August 4, 1846

Today I begin writing on the pages of this beautiful new book. My teacher presented it to me on my thirteenth birthday. I never expected to receive such a precious gift! It makes me feel that I am special. I love the book's soft leather binding and the red edge on the pages.

I don't worry that someone else will read it out here on the Canadian prairies. Papa is a voyageur and never learned to read much. My brother Pierre is eight and reads hardly at all. Little brother Armond is only four.

"I want you to have this book that came all the way from France," my teacher said when she pressed it into my hands. "You might like to write a journal of your experiences this year. You are very helpful to me and my sister when we need to know the meaning of Ojibwe words. After we've learned more words, my sister and I hope to print a small Ojibwe Indian dictionary." She opened my book and wrote on the first page:

August 4, 1846

For Josette Dupre on her birthday
From her teachers, Angelique and Marguerite Nolin

"Thank you, mademoiselle," I said, and curtsied the way she taught us in class. I stumbled as I raised my head, and I noticed I was almost as tall as her. My hands shook a little as I accepted this special present. I was so excited! I feel honored to have been chosen as the helper for the two Nolin sisters. They're the teachers here in St. Eustache, west of the Red River Settlement. They have asked me to translate Ojibwe words the other students use. I'm glad that I learned to speak Ojibwe from Mama when I learned to talk. I know French because it's the language we use at school, and Papa speaks it, too.

I miss my dear mama so very much. It's been five months now since she died, and sometimes people forget I'm not entirely grown up. They say I do a good job of washing and cooking for the boys and Papa. And my teachers treat me as if I'm not just another student. I'm so happy that I live in St. Eustache, where there is a school with such good teachers. Many girls never have the chance to go to school at all.

Wednesday, August 5, 1846

I usually walk home from school with my best friend, White Cloud, so we can talk.

"Oh, Josette, I wish I knew French as well as you do." White Cloud's voice sounded sad. "Sometimes I can hardly understand what the teachers are saying." I knew this because her parents speak only Ojibwe. "I want to learn more English words, too," White Cloud said.

After school she watches her baby brother, and I often sit with her while my brothers play outside. After Mama died this spring, Papa did not leave to be a steersman for a voyageur brigade as he did every other year. Instead he stayed at our cottage near the Assiniboine River, looking sad and forlorn and watching Armond while Pierre and I are at school.

White Cloud brought her brother outside, hung his cradleboard from a branch, and said, "How do you say . . . ?" She gave her brother's cradleboard a little push and looked to me for the French and English words.

"Do you mean *bébé*? That's 'baby.'" I said. "Or do you mean *frère*? That's 'brother.'" I gave the cradleboard another push. "Or do you mean *poussée*? That's 'push.'" We both laughed as the cradleboard rocked from the tree branch. "I don't know very many English words, either. All my classes are in French, the same as yours," I said. "I've just picked up a little from listening to the Scotch and English traders."

One thing I haven't told White Cloud is what Mlle Marguerite said to me one day, but I think of it often. "After the dictionary is ready, and you've finished our school here, my sister and I would like to send you to the school we attended in Montreal," she said. She told me it was a grand place with many big buildings, much larger than St. Boniface. The two sisters have fine manners and speak French so well that they sometimes seem out of place here.

Marguerite Nolin is friendly and very pretty, with her black hair pulled back and caught with a jeweled clip. Men always bow to Mlle Marguerite, and she smiles and laughs at them. They bow to Mlle Angelique, too, but she is in charge of the school, and more serious.

On their shelves they have many books. They read plays by Molière, novels by Victor Hugo, and many books of poetry. A new book by Alexandre Dumas, *The Three Musketeers,* has just arrived from France. As soon as they finish it, they will let me read it.

Both sisters wear long dresses of beautiful fabric that seem more appropriate for a fine city than a little frontier town. Their skirts are made of shiny black cloth. Both teachers are very nice, but Marguerite Nolin is my favorite. There is a sweet-smelling fragrance around when I stand close to them, trying to translate French words into Ojibwe. Mlle Marguerite explained it is eau de cologne that was sent to them from Paris. They rub a drop on their skin, and it stays fresh-smelling all day.

I asked Mlle Marguerite if she and her sister were French.

"No, we are Métis," she answered. "We came from the East with our family when our father moved to Sault St. Marie. My sister and I came here to St. Eustache to start a school. Our family is all Métis—descendants of French fur traders and Indian women. You are Métis, too, Josette. Your mother was Ojibwe, and your father is French and Indian. Be assured, Josette, it's a heritage to be proud of."

I've remembered what she said that day—about who I am, and, most of all, about school. I do know that some people in the Red River Settlement look down on the Métis.

Today at school the Nolin sisters and I laughed about Ojibwe words. I had told them that the Ojibwe word for "blueberries" was *minan*. Then they asked, are cranberries a similar word?

"No, cranberries are *mashkigminikan*," I said. They thought that long word was funny. Whenever I'm daydreaming, I remember what Mlle Marguerite said about going to school in Montreal someday.

Sometimes, though, I feel that I'm not able to do everything that people expect of me, especially taking care of my brothers. It's hard getting Pierre to pay attention when I ask him to do something. I'm not grown-up yet and don't want so many responsibilities at home all the time.

This book is so nice and the paper so fine that I was almost afraid to write in it. Now that I've started, though, I don't want to stop. I'll take it with me wherever I go.

Thursday, August 6, 1846

We live in a little cottage Papa built in the settlement of St. Eustache. It's about halfway between St. Boniface and the village where Mama's relatives live.

Our house is on a long strip of land going back from the river and into the woods. We tie up a canoe in front of the cottage. Behind the cottage we plant corn, squash, and beans, and keep an ox and a few chickens.

Until this year Papa worked every spring and summer as a voyageur, moving all kinds of goods by canoe to trading posts. There beaver and other furs that Indians had trapped during the winter are collected. I think he misses the voyageur life, being the steersman for eight or ten men, singing rhythmic songs to keep up the pace as they paddle in their big canoe. At night they would eat, make music, and dance to exercise their cramped legs.

Papa is getting old to be a voyageur. Sometimes portages between streams are very long. Each voyageur has to carry two ninety-pound packs on his back. The paths on portages have become too steep and slippery for him. This spring and summer Papa has been sitting at home brooding.

Friday, August 7, 1846

Last night we were sitting at the table looking out at the river that flows by our cottage. The boys had been teasing each other and running around the table. I was feeling that maybe I could get used to our life here without Mama, even though it would be hard.

Then Papa broke in, "Josette, it's time that we get away from here for a while." The boys stopped to listen. "I think it's time we go back to St. Boniface for a few days. We'll buy supplies and visit my sisters again."

We haven't been to St. Boniface since Mama died. I was born there, and it's the biggest town I've ever been to. Papa's family all live in St. Boniface. It's the French part of the Red River Settlement.

Then Papa had another idea. "After we get back, we could go west and camp with your Mama's relatives during the wild-rice harvest. It would be about time for it. Would you like that?" Papa knew we would. We love to go to *manominike* with Mama's side of the family. It's a family reunion and wild-rice harvest combined.

"Yeah, yeah!" shouted Pierre, who raised his fists above his head in glee. This was exciting news for the boys. When I went to bed, I cried myself to sleep because Mama wouldn't be with us.

Saturday, August 8, 1846

As I packed this morning I came across many things that reminded me of Mama. I couldn't help but think about the hard times we've been through.

This spring, when Mama felt labor pains starting, she took us back to her village to be with her mother. We call her Nokomis, which is "grandma" in Ojibwe. When the time came, Mama and Nokomis went by the river, where soft, dry grass grows, and stayed there all night. In the morning they came back with the new baby wrapped on a cradleboard to show to me and the boys. I lifted Armond so he could see the little bundle that was our new sister. The air was cool, so Nokomis had covered the baby's shoulders with cattail silk and soft squirrel skins. The bottom part of the cradleboard was stuffed with dried swamp moss, which could be thrown out when the baby wet it.

The baby was very quiet as we traveled home. Mama's long strokes moved us swiftly through the water. I had a chance to hold the baby and study her tiny fingers and little wrinkled face. She was so tiny and precious. I sang a little lullaby that I'd heard Mama sing, "Ba Ba, Se, Se," with no real words, as she paddled. Armond and Pierre wanted to play with her, too, but it is hard to stay still in a birch-bark canoe. When we got home, Mama took off the squirrel skin and put a soft white shirt on the baby.

"Sometimes we'll use moss in the cradleboard in the old way, but sometimes we'll use a soft diaper," Mama said.

She said an elder would come over after Papa came home, and we'd have friends over for a naming ceremony and feast. By then the elder would have had time to dream a spirit name for the baby. Mama gave the baby a French name, as she has done with each of us. We called her Amilie.

At home Amilie started to fuss and cry, and had trouble keeping Mama's milk down. Mama mixed water with dried cedar to make a special drink for her. No matter what we did, the baby kept on fussing. Mama started to feel sick, too.

She was so worried that the baby did not have an Ojibwe name yet that she asked a neighbor to do the naming ceremony without a feast. She was given the name Clear Sky as her spirit name. Mama sent a messenger to ask Nokomis to come to our house.

When she came the next day with an herb potion, the baby was too weak to swallow it. Mama held Amilie most all the time, and I fixed food for the boys. By the next morning the baby's skin was gray and she had stopped breathing. Mama's skin was hot, and she was inconsolable. She had lost a baby before Armond was born, too.

Nokomis made a bundle of the baby's clothes and gave the package to Mama to cradle in her arms. She said that was an Ojibwe custom that would make Mama feel better. Mama lay with the baby bundle all day.

Nokomis took little Amilie outside. The boys and I watched as she buried her in a birch-bark box, saying prayers to the Great Spirit. With soot from the bottom of a pan, she blackened our faces and told us we should stay near her until we had a dream, even if we had to stay all night.

I felt so sad, I wasn't sure what to do. Mama didn't want to get up at all. Nokomis made wild-rice gruel for her to eat, but she barely tasted it.

"Eat something, Mama," Pierre said. Armond and I pleaded with her, but she turned her head away. I put my hand on her forehead and could tell she had a fever. I did not know if that was because she was sad, or because she was getting sicker. Nokomis made more potions for Mama, but she was no better. I was in despair. I tried to be strong for Mama's sake, but I really wanted to cry; for her, for the boys, for Papa, for all of us.

It was almost dark when we heard Papa's voice as he rounded the bend of the river. He jumped from the canoe and bounded up the steps to see us, expecting the boys to greet him with laughter. They met him with the terrible news. Then Papa saw that Mama was lying on the bed, listless and sick. He rushed to her bedside and knelt beside it. After he stood up, he seemed both angry and frightened.

"Get some things packed now," he said to me in a rough voice. "As soon as it's light, we'll go to St. Boniface. There must be a doctor there who can help Mama."

I was so relieved that Papa was back. Papa asked Nokomis to go with us, but she shook her head sadly. She had never in her life been to St. Boniface. She gathered her things to begin the journey back to her village. I know she wanted to take Mama to the Ojibwe healers.

While I was remembering these things, I looked out the window through Mama's handmade curtains. I could not stop the tears from coming. What would happen to us now?

Sunday, August 9, 1846

This all happened months ago, but it's still fresh in my mind. I'm writing it down so I won't ever forget it.

For travel to St. Boniface, I fixed a bed for Mama on the floor of the oxcart and made it as soft and comfortable as I could. Papa carried her out to the cart, and we left before it was even light. When we got there, Papa took us to Aunt Germaine's house until Mama could be nursed back to health.

Aunt Germaine had heard that nurses called the Gray Nuns had arrived from Montreal a few months before. Papa asked them to come over to see Mama that afternoon. The nuns bathed her with cool water to make her more comfortable and said a rosary. The gray dress and white headdress of their habit put us at ease. Before they left the house, they showed me how to wipe Mama's skin to bring down her fever. They were kind and gentle to her, and spoke so reassuringly that I believed she would get better. Papa got a doctor as well, who assured us that the nurses were doing the best that could be done.

Next morning Papa sat by Mama, and Armond took naps at the foot of her bed. Pierre tried to tempt her with little bites of food, but she would not eat. I held her hand for hours, it seemed. The nurses came back the next afternoon, but she was not getting any better. We waited, watched, and hoped.

Mama seemed to be improving. The priest from the St. Boniface Church had come to Aunt Germaine's house. He baptized Mama and prayed for her.

That evening Mama spoke to each of us in turn.

"Be a good boy, and mind Josette," she told Armond. He nodded solemnly and tried to climb up on the bed beside her. I lifted him up to kiss her because the bed was too high for his four-year-old legs to reach.

Then she turned to Pierre. "You're growing up fast," she said. Usually so busy and mischievous, now he stood tall and straight next to the bed. "Learn from Papa. He can teach you many things." She looked to Papa with questioning eyes, and he put his hand on Pierre's shoulder.

After a few moments she turned to me, her sad eyes looking deeply into mine. "I'm glad you can help the teachers with Ojibwe words," she said. "You're almost grown now." She was quiet for a long time, and Papa nodded to us to let her rest. The boys and I waited in Aunt Germaine's parlor.

After a while Papa came to the doorway and said to me, "Mama asked for you." I went in and sat by the bedside as she slept. After a while she opened her eyes and smiled.

"Take good care of them, Josette," she said at last, and a few minutes later she stopped breathing.

After Mama died the priest came again. He prayed with all of us and said God would be with us. He helped Papa arrange for her burial at the St. Boniface cemetery. Great-Aunt Cecile and Aunt Germaine and all Papa's other relatives in St. Boniface came to the service.

We stayed the next few days and went over to her burial plot each day with flowers from Aunt Germaine's garden. One day I found Pierre sleeping by the flowers we put on the grave. Armond and I lay down beside her, too, remembering all she meant to us.

Now, months later, Armond still wakes during the night, crying for Mama. As I cuddle close to him, his tears wet my nightdress. After he falls asleep I sometimes cry myself to sleep, too. This has been hard to write down, but I want to be able to remember those sad days.

Tuesday, August 11, 1846

Last night Great-Aunt Cecile asked us over to her house for a special dinner. She used French recipes and her best China dishes. She roasted a duck, made pumpkin soup and maple syrup pie. She also baked a special sweet bread called *brioche.*

We'll have food for the rest of the week because Great-Aunt Cecile had also made meat pies called *toutiere* for us to take home. She showed me how to make brioche, but I don't always have yeast, butter, and eggs. Papa doesn't mind the bread we call bannock I make out of flour, water, and pork fat. It takes just a few minutes. At home that is what we usually eat for bread, along with wild rice and pemmican made from dried buffalo meat. This time of year food is plentiful because the garden is full of squash, corn, and two kinds of potatoes, white and sweet.

Wednesday, August 12, 1846

This morning I took Armond and Pierre over to see "the forks," where the Red River and the Assiniboine join. I remember the fun we had there at picnics with Papa's relatives before we moved. French people live on the east side of the river, and Scots live on the west side; but it's all called the Red River Settlement.

Papa took us in the oxcart to Fort Garry this afternoon. It's about ten miles north of the forks. There were guards in uniform at the gates and soldiers everywhere. Papa talked to some former voyageur friends who work there. Papa said he doesn't expect to work as a voyageur again. Since the Northwest Company and the Hudson Bay Company merged, there have been many changes. If we move to Fort Garry, it will be too far for me to go to school in St. Eustache. There must be a school near Fort Garry, too.

We bought salt and dried corn and peas before leaving for home. We don't need much, because our garden will be full of vegetables until frost comes. I tried to write as we rode in the oxcart, but I couldn't read the wiggly letters. Aunt Germaine gave me a piece of oilcloth to wrap around my beautiful book. I watched the dying sun descend as we traveled along the river. It was dark before we got back to our empty house in St. Eustache.

Saturday, August 15, 1846

I've been working in the garden and packing things away ever since we got back. We'll be gone for a while at the wild-rice harvest.

I put Mama's precious things, like her teapot and our old baby dresses, into a box and stored them in the loft. Papa told Uncle Phillipe that his family could stay at our cottage and take care of it while we're gone.

I still remember the floods in St. Boniface. During those scary days when the Red River rose over its banks, I helped Mama take the teapot and china cups to the church for safekeeping. The Red River flows north into the Hudson Bay, and ice up there lasts much longer than here. When the snow melts here, the water floods the flat land. Since we moved out by the Assiniboine River, we go west to Nokomis's village when it floods.

Today the boys and I put packages on our oxcart. Mlle Angelique says the oxcarts we use in Canada are a lot like carts that farmers use in France. The carts have two very large wheels that hold up a box. The box holds all the cargo, including the people. We use our ox to pull the cart, but some people use a horse.

Today the sun has been shining, and I washed

clothes. I put the tubs on a bench outside. While I was working, birds lit on the grass nearby, as though they were keeping me company. Mama always loved the smell of clothes after they had dried outside, and so do I. White Cloud came over, and we laughed as she helped me hang up our clothes.

Tomorrow we leave for the place where Nokomis's village stays for the wild-rice season. I told White Cloud we'll be there only two or three weeks if the rice is ripe. It's hard to guess exactly

It's a good thing I've been busy, because if I stop for a few minutes, I feel like crying. Pierre, big boy that he is, started wailing, "I want my Mama," last night when I asked him to go to bed; but I think it was mostly because he didn't want to go yet.

Armond was resting his head in his little arms on the table this afternoon and burst into tears. We all hate to leave this house because it reminds us of Mama.

Sunday, August 16, 1846

The bell sounded mournful as it called us to Mass this morning. Afterward we said good-bye to the priest and our friends. Then I went over to the school to say good-bye to my teachers. When we said we were going to the wild-rice harvesting, they were happy that we were going to spend time with Mama's relatives. Mlles Angelique and Marguerite Nolin will start school again after we come back from collecting wild rice. Many of their students help with the rice harvest.

The teachers were excited because Father Frederick Baraga, a priest traveling through this area, is collecting information about Indian languages. Father Baraga is compiling a large list of Ojibwe words, much bigger than the one I have helped on. Father Baraga already had a short version of his dictionary printed in France. He keeps enlarging his list, which he calls the "Otchipwe" language. That's the way he thinks the natives pronounce it.

"We'll need you as soon as you get back," Mlle Marguerite said. "We're helping him understand and define more words." I said we'd be back long before winter sets in. As we parted, she handed me the copy of *The Three Musketeers* she had promised I could borrow. She also gave me a small book of children's stories to read to the boys. Besides that I have a book of prayers, a Bible, a notebook, and of course, my precious journal to take along on our trip.

As I put things away at home many things reminded me of Mama's warmth and kindness. I miss her so much. I mull over in my mind the time that Papa took us to St. Boniface to get medical help. It didn't do any good.

2. We Stay with Nokomis for Manominike

Monday, August 17, 1846

We left home this morning and reached Nokomis's village by afternoon. Nokomis and all her relatives are camped in a shady grove near two lakes, preparing to harvest wild rice. The Ojibwe call this grain that grows in the water *manomin,* but at home we call it by the French word *folle avoine.*

When Nokomis heard our squeaking cart, she came out to greet us with outstretched arms. The boys and I jumped off as soon as Papa stopped the ox.

"My precious daughter's children," Nokomis said as she hugged Armond and Pierre. We hadn't seen her since the day she left our little cottage, but Papa had sent a message from St. Boniface to let her know about

Mama. Nokomis hugged me, too, and said, "You're so tall now, Josette, like your mama when she was young. She was like an *ogema.*" She always makes me feel that I'm her special granddaughter. Although she looked sad when we arrived, I felt she was very happy that Papa had brought us.

"Let me show you this new lodge where you can sleep," Nokomis said. Sheets of birch bark had been laid over a rounded frame made of saplings to form the walls. Over the top the largest sheets of birch bark made a rainproof roof. The inside was fragrant from cedar branches spread to make a soft bed. I knew we would love sleeping there. During wild-rice season all our aunts and uncles come for *manominike.* Every family works together on the big bags of wild rice to take home. It's the main food during the winter, and will even last from one season to the next. Even the children help.

Every evening we all sit around the fire and tell stories. We have a lot of fun with our cousins at manominike.

Papa has been talking to our uncles and making plans. He has decided we'll leave early to go to the fall buffalo hunt. I don't know much about buffalo hunting. I just hope this doesn't delay our going back to St. Eustache for too long. I don't want to miss school.

Thursday, August 20, 1846

Just as I did last year at the manomin harvest, I paddled through the shallow waters as Nokomis leaned stalks of wild rice over the canoe and tapped the ripe rice grains with a stick. We collected them in the bottom of the canoe.

"Careful, Josette, birch-bark canoes tip very easily," she said. We worked most of the morning until the boat was low in the water. Then we carefully tipped the canoe over, and the rice fell onto a blanket.

Saturday, August 22, 1846

The weather was sunny today. There are many children for Armond to play with this year. I don't have to watch him much. Cousin Little Bear played butterfly hide-and-seek with him for hours. Pierre was happy because he got to steer Auntie's canoe through the rice bed. Nokomis and I put the wild rice in pots over a blazing fire and stirred until the husks were dried.

She handed me a stick and said, "Now stand as far back as you can, but stir. Keep stirring. Don't let the rice scorch." Soon I felt like I was going to burn up!

After Nokomis said the rice had dried and cooled enough, the mothers and children put on clean moccasins and took turns stomping on it in a big tub to loosen the husks. I would have liked to do that, but Nokomis had other work for me.

"Come," she called. "Watch how this is done." She said to me, "I want to be sure you learn the old ways."

We took a shallow birch-bark basket full of wild rice, held it up high, and slowly poured it into another one on the ground to let the wind carry away the husks. It took a long time. I had to pour several times before all the husks had blown away. It was tiring.

As the sun began to set, the sky filled with beautiful colors of salmon and pink, and loons called to each other across the still water.

Sunday, August 23, 1846

Today Nokomis showed me a beautiful dress made of creamy tan deerskin, with moccasins and leggings to go with it. Then she said she had made it for me! I love the feel of the soft leather when I rub it against my cheek. I know that it has taken her weeks and weeks to make it. I tried it on and it fit me perfectly. She had also made a necklace of seeds and bone to wear with it. I did not tell her that in St. Boniface and St. Eustache we wear plaid, cotton dresses instead of deerskin. Cotton dresses can be easily washed when they get soiled. I will save this dress for special holidays when we visit Nokomis. I know I will treasure it always.

Later

I put on my new dress this evening to show our relatives. I curtsied to Nokomis to show my respect and thanked her for all her work. I walked around wearing it to show people what Nokomis had made. Everyone said I look like a real Ojibwe maiden in it. I know I look like Mama, but people can see that I am part French, too.

During the evening there were stories told and songs sung. We all begged Nokomis to tell a story just like she does at every family gathering. We sat around her on the ground as she spoke:

There was once a conversation between a weasel and a wolf.

"Let us have union in our families," said the weasel, "for my body is so feeble that I am obliged to hunt at night for fear of man, and get but a scanty living. Wolf, you often walk abroad by day, and men respect your courage and dexterity."

"True," replied the wolf, "but if I have courage, I also have strong enemies both day and night. A cousin of mine told me that wolves get fine sheep in the south; but in this poor country, we are lucky if we can catch a lynx or a rabbit, and I often go hungry, whereas your very feebleness is your protection. Be satisfied with what you are. You can catch mice and get grain or roots. The Creator has tempered our powers and appetites very well, and you often escape dangers that would crush me. Man is my worst enemy, and I am told a price is set on my head."

At this moment the trap of a hunter sprang, and the poor wolf was caught by the legs while the weasel scampered off.

Now Weasel and his grandchildren still hide in the woods and scamper quickly through the forest. Wolf comes down to the river to howl to the moon shining softly on the water. Both are proud of their powers but jealous of the other.

Nokomis knows many tales like this. Each has a lesson she wants her grandchildren to remember.

When she finished, all the cousins gathered about Papa and clamored for him to sing. He knows hundreds of songs that the voyageurs sing to keep rhythm as they paddle. He loves to entertain and show off, which embarrasses me. As he danced, he laughed and moved his arms as though he were paddling.

My canoe's of bark, light as a feather
That is stripped from silvery birch;
And the seams with roots sewn together,
The paddles white made of birch.

I take my canoe, send it chasing
All the rapids and billows acrost;
There so swiftly see it racing
And it never the current has lost.

It's when I come on the portage,
I take my canoe on my back,
Set it on my head topsy-turvy;
It's my cabin, too, for the night.

You are my voyageur companion;
I'll gladly die with my canoe,
And on the grave beside the canyon
You'll overturn my canoe.

People around the fire started to clap in time and sing with his rowing motions. It made him happy, too. It made me think about days long ago, long before Mama was sick. If Mama had been there, she would have shook her head at some of the songs he sang. She said they weren't for children's ears. Papa sang for a long time by the fire, and we all kept time by clapping hands. Then Uncle Painted Feather stood up and began to dance, first slowly, then faster and faster. Soon several other cousins began dancing. Everyone clapped and laughed.

Nokomis left the circle early. I think she was sad to see so much merriment. She thinks Mama might have survived if Papa hadn't taken her away.

The rice harvesting is not all done yet, but Papa decided we should be on our way to the buffalo hunt.

"If I shoot a buffalo, we'll have meat for most of the winter. With the rice we've gotten here, we'll have plenty of food," he said.

We were given the first bags of rice to take along. I protested to Papa that it was almost time for school to start and that the vegetables were still in the garden at home and needed to be brought in before the frost.

I remembered planting the garden with Mama in earlier years. This spring I had done it by myself. I cut potatoes into pieces and planted them with an eye looking up so that it would sprout into a new plant. I planted corn by dropping a few kernels into a hole along with a little fish, just like Mama used to do. When we left home, we had a tall stand of corn.

I knew that Nokomis would listen to me, so I told her how I felt about Mama's garden. Nokomis was sad, too. She said that gifts from Mother Earth should not be wasted. She put her warm hand on my shoulder and said she would ask a grandson to go with her after we left if it looked like the frost was coming. They will pick and store the things that can be kept for us, and use what won't keep. I feel so much better. I didn't want all my work to go for nothing.

Manominike ended with many happy-sad feelings for me because we knew we were still part of Mama's family, but it didn't feel quite the same as when she was here with us.

Monday, August 24, 1846

We left Nokomis's village this cloudy morning. She came out to the trail where she had met us before, to bid us good-bye. Pierre and Armond were sleepy from staying up late last night. I ran back to the bark lodge where we had stayed to be sure that the boys had not left anything. Some of our cousins were up and ran out to the cart to wave good-bye. Papa had attached the ox to the cart and was ready to leave. Nokomis had cooked some wild rice and shaped it into balls for us to share while we're traveling. She also packed a little lunch for later today. I knew Nokomis would deliver some wild rice to our house, too, when she went there to harvest the corn and other vegetables. We thanked her for taking care of us since Mama had left us.

"May the Great Spirit follow you on your journey into buffalo country," she said as she waved good-bye.

We traveled south all day through tall grass. There were almost no trees, and we stopped for the night at a bare place near the river. Papa showed Pierre how to build a fire on the ground. There were many saskatoon berries growing by the river. They are not nearly as sweet as blueberries. The boys helped me pick some for supper.

What we didn't eat, we will dry and keep in the back of the cart. They might be good to flavor our food later.

When Pierre asked Papa how long it would take to get to the place where the buffalo roam, he said, "Maybe three or four days. It depends on how fast we travel."

Three or four days sounds like a long time to me. After riding in the cart all day, Pierre and Armond were eager to play, tease, and jump around Papa. Armond wanted to know what a buffalo was. Papa told him it is a very big animal that has brown wool all over its body, and it looks a little like our ox, except it has a much bigger head, covered with shaggy hair.

It is not as though we are going on a long journey— Papa thinks it is like a vacation. I am curious to see the buffalo, too. Nokomis said she saw them many times when she was younger.

"But will they chase us?" Armond asked.

"I've never heard that they chase people," Papa said. "We're not the only people going. There will be many Métis from the Red River Settlement there, too." He told us even Scotch settlers go these days, because crops have been so poor. The dried buffalo meat lasts for years after it has been prepared, he said.

We ate some of the food Nokomis sent along—

smoked fish, bannock, and for a treat, pieces of maple sugar.

Tonight as Papa sat smoking his pipe, he announced he was giving up the life of a voyageur to take care of his motherless children. He's said that before; but being a voyageur is the only work he's ever done, and I know he misses it.

After everyone else has gone to sleep, I have time to think and write. I hope this trip to the buffalo hunt does not take many days so that we can go home to St. Eustache for school soon. Papa makes such rash decisions. He says I'll learn a lot at the hunt, but I think not. It will be exciting for Pierre, and I'll have to watch Armond. He's curious, and I can't depend on cousins like I could at the rice harvest.

Last night I had a most surprising dream. I dreamed I lived in Montreal among tall and beautiful buildings. I was a student at a very fine school, like the one the teachers probably went to. We were very proper students who wore silk dresses and carried parasols to shade us from the sun when we went for a walk. We curtsied when we met ladies and gentlemen. In the afternoon we drank tea out of delicate china cups. Everyone spoke French. We rode in fine carriages instead of carts.

Just when I was enjoying this lovely dream, one of the teachers asked me to translate an Ojibwe word into French; and when I couldn't remember it, I woke up with a start.

My most dreaded thought is that now I won't ever be able to finish school or help with the dictionary, and the Nolin sisters won't send me to Montreal to school. Even if I do get to Montreal, will I be able to speak French well enough to pass as a real lady? Papa is so carefree about this trip, and I know the buffalo hunt will give us meat for winter, meat that we need; but I wish we weren't going. We're traveling away from all we know. The teachers won't even know where to find me.

Thursday, August 27, 1846

It was very hot today as we traveled south. There were no trees for shade. We camped close to the river. Pierre plunged straight into the water with a shout. No one was around us, so Armond and I followed. We felt so cool and refreshed, we called to Papa to jump in, too.

We ate some of the cooked wild rice Nokomis had sent along for us. Papa made a smudge fire to keep the mosquitoes away, but it didn't help much. I have lots of itching bites, and Armond has big red lumps on his little arms. After eating, we looked for berries. I hoped to find some blueberries, but they grow under trees, and there aren't many trees around here. Since there were plenty of saskatoon berries growing along the river, we all ate our fill.

Papa says he thinks we will cross the border into the United States today. There is no marker to show where the thirty-ninth parallel is, and nobody around here knows where it is. When we get to the Pembina trading post, we'll go west to where the hunt begins.

3. We Become Part of a Buffalo Hunt

Saturday, August 29, 1846

We arrived at Fort Pembina this afternoon. I expected a large building, but it's just a small trading post put up last year by Norman Kittson. Papa knew him when he was a voyageur. Kittson said the hunt is going to be more organized than it used to be and pointed west to where the hunters have camped.

Papa talked to him for so long that we had to hurry to get to the buffalo camp before nightfall. When we got there, we found big clusters of tents, carts, and hundreds of people gathered.

We looked around for some time before we found a good place for the cart. Most of the good ones were already taken. Finally Pierre spotted one; and when we stopped there, two young men named Charley and Stan helped us get our cart into the circle. That was generous of them because they'll have less room for themselves now.

Afterward I took Armond by the hand, and we walked around a few of the circles of parked carts. The smoky air smelled of roasting partridge. Many friendly strangers greeted us. Women as well as men relaxed around their fires, laughing and talking.

After the ox was fed and watered, Papa went looking for familiar faces. He found Frank Mousseau, a man he used to know in St. Boniface. We finished the food Nokomis sent, and then walked around the camp until we found his cart. We met his wife, Francine, and their children. Stephan is eight, the same age as Pierre, and they became friends right away. Marie is ten, and Louis and Eliza are younger, and they all wanted to play with Armond.

Sunday, August 30, 1846

Today I have plenty of time to write and read because the hunt hasn't started yet. I opened the Bible and found Psalm 8. When David wrote it, he felt far away from friends and very small as he looked up at the heavens. I'm glad I'm not the only person who feels like that. I wish I had brought more books along, even though the Bible would keep me busy for a long time. I'm going to read *The Three Musketeers* from cover to cover before we get home. I know the teachers would have loaned me other books if I had asked.

Other women and children wait by their carts like we do. Armond is racing around camp, asking questions. It is very hard to keep track of him.

Monday, August 31, 1846

Today Papa went to a meeting of the men who are going to hunt. I felt strange and lonely in the cart surrounded by people, mostly men. The boys and I went over to the Mousseau wagon to get acquainted. Francine told me she's thirty-two, the same as Mama would be. To her this trip is an adventure for the family, and they're all looking forward to the excitement. Francine said most of the Métis are here to put up meat for the winter. If they get extra, they will be able to sell it.

"Women and children do not go out to chase the herd. We just wait in the camp until some buffalo are killed," she said. "Then they'll send back scouts to tell us where they are, and we'll take our carts out there to dress the meat."

I don't care to see animals slaughtered, but I wish I could ride a horse out to see the buffalo stampede. I don't want to wait here till all the excitement is over.

Tonight Pierre told Papa he wanted to hunt buffalo.

Papa looked at him and said, "The men who plan the hunt make the rules because there have been arguments before. I know one thing: You're not old enough to go."

"I'm not? But what will I do?" Pierre protested.

Papa said, "You and Stephan need to stay here and patrol the camp. That's a big responsibility. Animals, like wolves, could sneak up to eat our food. Dakota Indians live around here. They might be curious. You boys need to keep a close lookout." Pierre had a scowl on his face.

"To hunt, you have to be able to shoot while you're riding a horse. The horses don't go the direction you expect. The buffalo are running as fast as they can. It's very easy for a man to get shot." Papa stopped to be sure that Pierre was really listening. Then he added, "There was a time, when I was younger, that we could get close enough and shoot from the ground. Now it's all done on horseback, and we don't even have a horse. I'll be lucky if I can borrow one."

Pierre kicked at the wheels of the cart and pouted until he went to bed.

We've heard tales of buffalo hunts all our lives from men smoking their pipes with Papa around the campfire. They told about the days when the buffalo herds were so large that they could watch a herd go by all day, and still more buffalo would keep coming. I don't blame Pierre for wanting to be part of the excitement.

Tuesday, September 1, 1846

Stephan told Pierre that he can ride one of their ponies. They brought it along for Marie, their oldest girl, to ride. He is excited. The boys asked if they could ride alongside the hunters if they stayed clear of the men and their horses, but Frank and Papa said no.

I talked to a woman named Adele, who is a Dakota Indian. Her husband is Métis. She has been on many hunts. She explained how she carves up the meat and pulls out the bloody, slimy guts. The guts are saved to make bags and cords. She says every part of the buffalo is used for something. Adele reminds me of Nokomis, but without her gentleness. She will show Francine and me how to cut and dry the meat when we get it. I can't imagine doing any of this myself.

Adele is teaching me Dakota words while we work. She calls the buffalo *tatanka*, but the buffalo robes are *ptehasina*. *Htani* is work. I found blueberries under the trees, and Adele called them *aunyeyapi*. When I see most anything, like a bird or a birch tree, I ask the word for it in Dakota. It's fun to learn those words that are different from Ojibwe.

Did Papa know that I would have to carve up buffalos? I don't think Mama ever went on hunts. Who prepared the meat then? Maybe the Nolin sisters became teachers so that they didn't have to butcher buffalo.

Wednesday, September 2, 1846

A man named Marcel will loan Papa a horse. Papa said to me, "We'll leave the ox with the cart in camp, and you can bring it out when we have our first luck hunting." Pierre or I will have to take the ox to graze and to the creek for water every day. I'm not looking forward to any of this.

At the meeting yesterday Papa learned there are over a thousand carts here, four hundred men and over eight hundred women and children. Most have been on hunts before and have brought extra carts to bring back the meat. The hunters are divided into teams with captains. Papa asked me to read a paper to him on the rules of the hunt:

No. 1: No buffalo to be run on the Sabbath day.
No. 2: No party to fork off, lag behind, or go before, without permission.
No. 3: No person to run buffalo before the general order.
No. 4: Every captain with his men, in his turn, to patrol the camp and to establish night patrols.
No. 5: For a trespass against these laws, the offended will have his saddle and bridle cut up.

Thursday, September 3, 1846

Last night around the campfire, the campers sang and danced for hours. Fiddlers played French songs that we know. The dancing was like home, too, with two lines of dancers facing each other. They played, "If you will come and dance with me, a feathered cap I'll give to thee," with many more verses that I had never heard before. Then they started, "At the clear running fountain. . . . I bathed without delay," and each time the refrain, "Your love long since overcame me, ever in my heart you'll stay." Some of the young men were acting silly, and pretended they were fainting when they looked at the girls.

Francine persuaded me to dance because there weren't enough women taking part. It gave me a chance to get a good look at the people in camp. I saw there were many young men lined up to dance, including Charley and Stan from the next cart. Some men were very flirtatious and winked when we clapped or twirled.

I noticed a tall young man that was in the dance. Every time we faced each other in the line, he gave me a big smile. He is very handsome, with striking features and dark hair. While others shouted over the music, he just kept dancing and smiling. I had such a good time. It reminded me of parties we had in St. Eustache. Mama and Papa used to dance at them, and even I did last year. Those happy days are gone now, but I still enjoy the songs.

Papa and I carried the sleeping boys back to our cart, and I lay down thinking about the happy time we had tonight among strangers.

Friday, September 4, 1846

Last night three scouts were appointed to search for the buffalo. We waved as they left this morning. The hunters are excited and anxious to get going.

The women, carts, and children will need to wait until the hunters have found the buffalo, killed some of them, and sent the scouts back to tell us where they are. I hope the old men who are supposed to stay with us on patrol know what to do if wolves come.

Sunday, September 6, 1846

The thunder of hooves and gunshots woke me this morning. The scouts rode in and shot guns into the air to rouse the hunters. They had found a large buffalo herd.

The sun was bright as the hunters on horseback lined up in formation, as though they were going to battle. Horses stamped and snorted impatiently. Papa picked up his gun and saddled the horse he had borrowed from Marcel. Then he tossed Armond in the air and gave him a big squeeze.

"Wish us luck!" he called to Pierre.

The air bristled with excitement. The scouts in the

lead held blue flags aloft that snapped in the breeze above the hunters' heads. When the order was given, they rode off with a shout. Dust rose from the ground, and the earth shook with the thundering of hooves. Pierre, Armond, and I stood with the women and children, waving handkerchiefs and cheering. It was a thrilling sight. I sneezed as dust blew across our faces. We stood there until the whole group of riders became tiny flecks on the horizon.

As we were waiting a girl named Sophie started talking to me. She is from the Red River Settlement so it will be fun to get to know her. Both her older brother and father are hunters. We talked for a while, but Armond kept pulling my arm, so I told her where our cart was parked. On the way back we passed Francine's cart.

"Have you seen Stephan?" she asked. I told her no, not since the hunters left. As Armond and I kept walking, I wondered what could have happened to Pierre. By afternoon Francine was back by our cart, looking worried.

"Both the ponies are gone," she said. Francine and I assumed the boys followed the hunters. There are so many. Will they find Papa among them? Or will they be so afraid that they will hide from him? Francine said she had asked the two older men who patrol the camp and the women in camp whom she saw to be on the lookout for them. We have such a disadvantage because the boys have the ponies, and we will have to search on foot.

I said I could look for the boys myself. Francine offered to watch Armond so I could go. I told her I would check down by the creek, where we water the ox, and then follow it to the west. I had hoped Francine and I would get acquainted, but not this way.

At sunset I returned to camp without having found the boys. Armond fell asleep as we talked about what to do next. As darkness fell several women who had been helping us look came back to join us by the fire. I went to bed but could not fall asleep. Every little sound startled me. I worried about what Papa would say. I tried not to think about animals that could harm the boys.

Monday, September 7, 1846

This morning I took Armond, still asleep, over to Francine's cart. Then I struck out on another search. I tried to imagine what I would have done if I were Pierre. As I walked along the creek, I listened carefully. In the snap and crackle of sticks as I stepped through the bushes, I could pick out the sounds of birds. No crying of little boys. I walked and listened for hours without success.

When I came up from the creek on my way back to camp, I heard a strange noise. I turned and saw two horses, grazing in the distance. As I got closer, they looked like the ponies the boys would have been riding! I was frightened. Where were Pierre and Stephan? Should I go back to camp for help? Or get on one of the ponies and see where it would take me?

Then an Indian man with a bow and arrow came up through the brush near the creek only minutes behind me. I was surprised there had been another person down there. When I spoke to him in Ojibwe, he ignored me. Then I tried a few words in Dakota. "*Tatanka wanase?*" He seemed to know that meant "buffalo hunt." I said I was looking for two *hoksiidan* and with my hand motioned how tall the boys were. I knew he understood me when he motioned for me to follow him. I was hoping it would not be some sort of a trap. He strode briskly through the brush, and I followed.

Not far away on a cave ledge under an overhang, the boys were sitting. Their faces were smeared with muddy tears. Both boys looked frightened. Pierre was crying. When he saw me, he held up his arm. I was furious and filled with relief at the same time.

"You boys have got yourselves into a lot of trouble,"

I said. Pierre started making louder sobs, and I said, "Come down and show me what's wrong with your arm." Pierre shook his head, but he did come down.

"Your mother is very worried about you," I said to Stephan in a cold, even voice. I was too exasperated to scold.

"The ponies started to run," said Stephan. "Pierre isn't used to riding, so he fell off. I slid off my pony, too, when they started to go fast."

The boys were too frightened to put up a fight when I said we were going back to camp. They followed me, and I motioned to the Indian hunter to come with us, too. We stopped by Adele's cart on the way to find Francine. Adele talked with the man in Dakota. The boys ran to Francine's cart while Adele, the Dakota man, and I followed. Adele explained that the man's name was Lonely Thunder.

"He was hunting early this morning and found a little black bear up in a tree. The boys were by their ponies, trying to persuade the bear to come down. Lonely Thunder motioned to them to be cautious because the mother bear might be close by," Adele said. "The ponies were startled, and your brother fell off."

By the time we got to Francine's wagon, the two

boys were nowhere in sight. Francine explained that the ponies had returned on their own. I started to tell her what Adele had said, and the boys came out.

"We saw this baby bear in a tree, and we were trying to get it to come down," Stephan said. "Then the ponies started to run."

"When the man came out of the woods, he must have scared them," said Stephan.

"Where were you during the night?" I asked.

"We stayed under a ledge where nothing could find us," Stephan explained. "We wanted to come home, but it was dark. We were scared. We saw lots of things moving around before we fell asleep. A groundhog came there and went into his hole. And then a chipmunk came by to peek at us."

"Didn't you think we'd be worried?" Francine asked.

"We did, Mama. We did." Stephan said, and both boys nodded.

"Pierre's arm might be broken," Adele said. "Let me look," she coaxed. Adele and Lonely Thunder both examined the arm. They agreed it was broken. It was a slow process with Lonely Thunder explaining it all to Adele, who then told me.

"Lonely Thunder has set a broken arm before,"

Adele said. "He will fix it." I told Pierre that he must let them touch it. Adele held his shoulder and arm in her hands. Pierre screamed when Lonely Thunder pulled hard on his wrist. Adele explained he had to pull the arm to set the bone in place. Pierre hollered some more, but Adele explained it needed to be set before it started to heal so that Pierre would not have a crippled arm. At last Lonely Thunder felt sure that the bone was back in place. He asked Stephan to bring him a small, flat board from a crate. He tied this board to Pierre's arm, saying he needed to keep it tied there for a few weeks until the bone healed. Adele made a sling from a piece of cloth.

"Now, that's better, isn't it?" I asked. He nodded un-certainly.

"It still hurts, though," he said.

The boys were subdued all day and took naps in the afternoon.

Later

Sophie came over this evening. She says she's glad that she found someone who doesn't just talk about chil-dren and having babies.

I admire Sophie's wavy dark hair and creamy-smooth, perfect skin. It's so beautiful. Not like my straight black hair and tanned skin. She said that she is the only girl in her family.

"That's why my brothers call me 'the little princess,'" she said with a smile that showed her dimples. Her grandfather came out to the Red River from Montreal. She thinks she's mostly French, with just one Indian great-grandmother.

Tuesday, September 8, 1846

Sophie went with me to explore the canyon today. We found some black raspberry bushes by the creek. Mama always called them black caps. They're getting a little dried out by this time of year, but they'll still be good to flavor things I bake, like bannock or pancakes.

"I don't know much about cooking," Sophie said. "My mother always does it." She stayed to eat with us. She liked the taste of the bannock biscuits.

"Will you teach me how to make these?" she asked.

I said I would, but I don't know much about cooking, either. "My great-aunt Cecile in St. Boniface has offered to teach me how to make many fancy dishes," I said. I told Sophie that I thought she'd help her, because they live near each other. I promised to send a note with Sophie to Great-Aunt Cecile so that Sophie can visit her.

Wednesday, September 9, 1846

Two scouts returned to camp late this morning to
tell us about the first two days' hunt. A large number of
buffalo were killed. We hurried to gather our belongings
and put out the morning fires. I have kept our packets of
clothes on the wagon so we would be ready to move.
The two boys were willing to help with everything.

We made a big procession as we followed the scouts
with our carts, oxen, ponies, and children. I had to drive
the ox. The sky above us was bright blue with whiffs of
puffy clouds moving across it.

The scouts led us to a place where dead buffalo lay all
around on the ground. Their great bodies were on their
sides, and one lifeless eye stared up at us. Papa saw us right
away and pointed out the one that he thought he killed. I
keep telling myself it would be just like butchering a steer.
Of course, I have never done that myself, either.

When I told Papa that the boys had been gone, he
was upset and went right over to talk to Frank. Even

though I know what the boys did was a bad thing, I can't help but feel sorry for them.

Tonight the men ate and laughed loudly, bragging about how they had caught the buffalo herd by pursuing it in a circle and confusing the animals into chasing each other. The hunters stayed on the outside of the circle and aimed at them.

I saw a man who had a bad bullet wound in his leg. It's a wonder that only one hunter was shot. They're all shooting while riding on horseback and can't take time to aim. Several men were also injured when falling from their horses, and two horses had to be destroyed because they were badly hurt. The one Papa borrowed is still all right, and I am thankful because he would have had to pay for it otherwise.

After supper Papa and Frank took the boys aside to question them. They hung their heads as they admitted they rode along with the group, but stayed out of sight. When the hunters stopped following the creek, the boys didn't dare follow. Frank, Francine, and Papa listened with pursed lips, shaking their heads.

"Don't you boys have consideration for anyone else?" Papa asked.

Tomorrow our work will begin. There is much to be done to store the buffalo meat.

At sunrise the men plan to gallop off for another day of hunting. Pierre and Stephan will take turns patrolling the camp again, after the men have left. A few older men will stay in camp, too. After all this effort we don't want our meat stolen by coyotes and wolves.

Thursday, September 10, 1846

We arranged our wagons so we could work together. Sophie, her mother, Francine, and I need to be near Adele, who is showing us how to cut the skin and woolly fur away from the meat. She told us to put the skin aside until we have taken care of the meat.

What a scene this is! Adele is doing so many things. She is tending the injured men because she is a Dakota medicine woman. She is also showing us what to do as she works on her own buffalo. Soon our arms and hands are covered with blood. Flies circle around our heads and land on our sticky arms. I am already exhausted from the cutting; but Adele never stops, so we keep going, too. Francine's daughter Marie helps her, even though she's only ten. Sophie and her mother work together. I'm the only one who doesn't have a helper. I really hate this sticky, smelly job. I can't help that it makes me feel like throwing up.

Friday, September 11, 1846

Today Sophie and I split a log in two so we would have flat places to work. After cutting the meat into chunks, we sliced it into thin slivers to make pemmican. Even though the cutting was bloody, Sophie and I could talk at the same time. The time went faster, but the smells and the insects kept getting worse. My arms and shoulders ached from shooing away flies with small leafy branches. I felt like a knife was stuck right between my shoulder blades.

Adele told us to make tall, wood cache racks to hang the slivers of meat from while it dries. Francine and I sent Pierre and Stephan to find small trees to use to build them. Armond followed the boys back and forth from the creek all day. I hope he'll fall asleep early tonight. Adele and Francine cut the buffalo meat into strips while Sophie and I hung the little strips of meat on the drying racks, where the hot sun dries it.

When Sophie and I quit work for today, we went down to the river to wash the blood spots out of our skirts. It seemed hopeless, so we took off our dresses, washed them completely, and hung them up on branches to dry. Then we took a dip in the river. It felt good after that hot, bloody work. Since our dresses were still wet and it was getting dark, we wore our underclothes back to camp. We didn't think anyone could see us, but then we heard Pierre, Stephan, and their friends giggling. Those spies!

Sophie showed me her sewing. She is making a trousseau for when she gets married. She has hemmed some little towels with very tiny, fine stitches, and now she is making beautiful lace on the ends. As she works on a towel, it's fun to watch the bobbin move in and out with the thread and watch the dainty lace appear. It is called tatting and is much more delicate than the crocheting Aunt Germaine does. Sophie promised to look in her sewing box for another bobbin and teach me how to tat.

Later Sophie and I walked to the river and sat under the trees, watching the water flow north toward our old homes. Sophie told me that her fiancé is here on the hunt, too.

"His name is Antoine, and we plan to be married when we get back home," she said. Her eyes sparkled as she spoke. She told me she has known him for years because they were in school together in St. Boniface. I wonder if I will ever meet anyone who will be as nice to me as Sophie says Antoine is to her. She loves him so. When the hunters come back in a few days, Sophie will bring him over so that I can meet him.

I envy Sophie because her plans for the future are settled. I'm only three years younger, and I don't know what's going to happen in my life. But at least we know that when we leave here, we have a home to go back to.

Saturday, September 12, 1846

Today Adele showed us how to boil down the fat. I used Mama's big kettle. It's a good thing the days are getting a little cooler because we've got fires everywhere—under the kettles and under the meat strips so they will dry faster. Pierre and Stephan built slow fires under each rack, using dried buffalo chips for fuel. There are plenty of droppings. This whole place has started to take on a strong, unpleasant odor.

"We must work fast because the hunters might bring back more buffalo tomorrow," Adele said. I can hardly bear to think of it.

Adele thinks the buffalo liver is especially delicious uncooked. She talked the boys and me into trying it. It tasted warm and fresh and a little chewy. Sophie wrinkled up her nose and wouldn't try it. We saved the buffalo tongue to have when Papa comes back because Adele says it is the very best part. I hope he enjoys it because I've had enough raw buffalo.

Sunday, September 13, 1846

This morning we were all still exhausted. Big iron kettles full of hot fat hung over fires on the ground. The children were running around and chasing each other. Suddenly Francine's little Eliza tripped. She fell hands down into a hot, smoldering fire.

"Mama, Mama," Marie called as she picked up her little sister. Eliza cried as she held out her ash-covered hands. Francine ran to them and washed off the ash.

Eliza's hands and arms are going to blister now, poor thing. We slathered grease on the burned places right away like Mama used to do.

Louis says Armond was chasing Eliza, so I went over to scold him. He said that they were just playing, and he wasn't chasing her toward the fires. I know that

Armond would never have hurt her on purpose, but Marie blames him anyway.

"Somebody has got to be watching a four-year-old," Francine said. Although she didn't say so, I feel that she blames me.

While the fat cooked down, Adele showed us how to scrape the hide to make buffalo-hide containers. It takes hours! Both sides have to be scraped—the one where the flesh of the animal was, and the other to remove the hair and wool. After that we mixed the buffalo brains with water and rubbed them on both sides of the hide. Adele says we have to keep working the hide for several days or it will get brittle. By "working" she means moving it around and around and kneading it until it is soft. All the children help, but four-year-olds won't keep at it very long.

I am uncomfortable talking with Francine because I feel guilty now. It's very hard to do all the work of cutting buffalo and still watch Armond. Sometimes I feel too much is expected of me.

4. A Scare in Camp

Monday, September 14, 1846

This afternoon we had a big scare. I felt a strange thundering from the ground and looked up. Oddly, there were no clouds. Then Sophie started to scream. People looked up, and then everyone screamed. A herd of buffalo was charging toward us.

"Watch out, Pierre! They're coming our way," I yelled. I grabbed Armond in my arms and threw him into the cart. My heart was pounding, and he was screaming.

When I yelled, Stephen and Pierre jumped on the ponies. I picked up a blanket and ran forward, flapping that blanket as hard as I could, trying to get the buffalo to veer off. The boys tried to do the same on their ponies. Then I grabbed one of the big flags of the Métis and waved it in both hands as the charging, sweating beasts came closer. They ran so hard, snorting as they came. I could hardly believe what I was seeing.

At the very last moment, the whole herd turned off to the side and headed south. They must have been diverted by the flag I was holding high and waving through the air with all my might. The ground shook with the pounding hooves. The stench of their warm fur coats was all that trailed behind.

While I stood there waving the flag Sophie had crawled into the cart to hold Armond. The women stood where they had been working, their knives and kettles in hand, as though that would protect them. Francine and Sophie hugged me. All the women said I did a great thing, but I only did what had to be done. Pierre and Stephan were very brave, too.

What if it hadn't worked? The boys love danger and excitement, but they could have been killed. The rest of us would have been, too. I shoved the flag back into its stand, where it was hoisted high to let anybody charging across the plains know that we're part of the Métis buffalo hunt.

"I've been on many a hunt," Adele said. "I've never seen this happen before." Although she had managed to stay calm, I think she had been afraid, too.

The buffalo pack sped into the distance, but a baby buffalo stayed behind. Its nose was close to the ground, and its tiny eyes were timidly darting about. After we all calmed down, the children in camp brought water and got close enough to pet it.

We all keep kneading our pieces of buffalo hide, to make them soft enough for making pouches. Our hands get tired. Stephan and Pierre even keep doing it while they patrol the camp. Everybody wants to rest after the day's scare.

I like it here at night when the camp is quiet and the children are sleeping. *Quiet* isn't really the right word. There are crickets. There is the sound of breathing. Children cry out in their sleep, and some people snore. Here in the flat Red River valley, the glow of the setting sun lasts for hours. There are no hills to hide behind. As the glow fades, the sky becomes alive with millions of stars.

Wednesday, September 16, 1846

When we got up this morning, the baby buffalo was nowhere in sight. The children looked all around the edges of the camp for it. I wonder if its mother came back looking for it.

Today Adele showed me how to punch holes in the buffalo hide with an awl, and then thread the cord through the holes to make bags. My fingers are stiff from sewing with rawhide laces. Next we took the dry meat, put it into the bags, and poured the fat over it. The pemmican stored this way keeps for a long time, even years, Adele says.

Sophie's mother gave me an extra buffalo skin that she doesn't need. It can be a carpet in front of the fire when we get back home. We've cut up some rawhide to use for rope, and Papa will use the horns to make into spoons and ladles later.

The nights are becoming cooler. Those of us who haven't finished with our meat and hides are staying up late tonight. After working for so many hours, we got a little silly. We started singing old voyageur songs, the bawdier the better. Adele knows lots of them. At least it kept a rhythm going and helped to get the work done.

Saturday, September 19, 1846

The hunters rode into camp late this afternoon. Sophie and I rushed out to greet them. Ahead of them was a scout with a man draped over the back of the saddle. When they got close, Sophie rushed over. It was Antoine.

"They stopped the chase as soon as I noticed that he was dragging on the ground," Papa said. "He was hit by a bullet. Some hooves trampled on his arm, too."

Sophie helped lift Antoine off the horse. I ran to find Adele. When we returned Adele reached into the wound with her fingers and pulled the bullet out. Then while Sophie cradled Antoine's head in her lap, Adele poured whiskey into the wound and on places where the skin was scraped off. It stung, but Antoine tried to smile. Oh, I feel sick inside for Sophie.

During the evening a group of us sat around the fire near Antoine. Everyone was melancholy. Papa began to tell about accidents he'd seen when he was a voyageur. Men often stumbled and fell into rivers as they tried to get past the rapids carrying big loads on their backs, he said. They used to drink and fight at night, too. I had not heard Papa talk this way about his work before. When we were younger I thought being a voyageur was a life of laughter and excitement. I wonder if Papa wanted to stop being a voyageur because so many of his friends died young.

Sophie tried to comfort Antoine all evening. Most of the time he was unconscious. Francine and Frank stayed in their tent. I know she's thankful Frank came back unhurt and wants the family to be all together this first night back.

Tomorrow a few carts will pick up the buffalo killed yesterday and bring them back so that the whole camp doesn't have to move again.

Wednesday, September 23, 1846

Most carts are loaded down with buffalo meat. Sophie and Antoine are leaving first. They will ride together in his father's wagon, and her family will follow. They'll go straight to the nuns in St. Boniface. Sophie and I sat up last night to talk. Whenever Antoine winced or murmured, Sophie jumped up to comfort him. Plans for her trousseau no longer seem important.

Thursday, September 24, 1846

Francine and Frank are leaving tomorrow. I think Francine is sorry for being so cross when Eliza fell, although Eliza is still suffering from her burns. Francine and Sophie have been like sisters to me. After our days of working together, I feel close to them. They can still be friends because they both live in St. Boniface, but we live too far away. Of course, none of us could have done our job without Adele. I will miss her, too.

Friday, September 25, 1846

Norman Kittson, the trader at Pembina, has come out to the camp a few times. He always comes by to talk to Papa. I have found out that Kittson has offered Papa a job as a teamster in his cart-train business, which takes furs and meat from the north down to St. Paul on the Mississippi River. Papa sounds pleased about it. However, I feel that Papa has betrayed my trusting nature.

"This would be a good way to travel," Papa said. "I'll be paid for it, and food is provided for the journey. We'll see a place we've never been to." Before I could even ask questions, he continued: "Kittson doesn't want all young drivers. He knows I'm used to managing a voyageur crew, being a steersman. This is the best time of year to travel, he says. It's not too hot, and the grazing is still good for the animals when we stop for the night. We'll get down there before winter sets in, and that's important."

This is not at all what I expected when we went to see Mama's relatives for the wild-rice harvest. What will happen to my job helping the teachers with the Ojibwe dictionary?

"If I do this, I'll be able to take you three along," Papa said. "I've already told Kittson that my wife died. We'll take this first trip between Pembina and St. Paul and see what happens. Maybe this will end up being a new kind of life for us." My heart sank when he added, "Josette, write a letter to Cousin Phillipe to tell him his family can stay in the house this winter. I'll find someone that's going back north to deliver it."

"Papa, I can't believe you would do this!" I cried out. "Pierre and I need to go back to school."

"You're a child, Josette. I have to find a way for our family to survive. Kittson offered me a chance to work. I thought you'd understand."

"Papa, you haven't been listening. I've told you many times what I want to do. To go back to school and work with the Nolin sisters," I said emphatically.

"I'm sorry, Josette. I still have to make the decisions in this family." *I will not cry. I will not cry,* I said to myself, and angrily walked down by the creek. I walked along the rushing water until dark, and came back to the cart after Papa and the boys were asleep.

Saturday, September 26, 1846

This morning there was a chill in the air that made me feel sad. Leaves were turning yellow down by the creek. Armond and I walked around the camp the way we did on the first day, but many of the wagons and tents were gone. Only the blackened remains of their fires were left behind.

I sat down between some of the willows by the river and had a good cry. I wondered if the teachers miss me as much as I miss them. I wondered if White Cloud was helping the teachers with Ojibwe words, even though she doesn't know French very well. Does she miss our talks? I keep thinking of all the friends I won't see this fall. It sounds like such a long journey all the way to St. Paul.

Overhead puffy white clouds move across the sky.

I look up and feel that Armond and Pierre and I are drifting with Papa down the Red River valley just like the clouds that float across the sky. What will we do when we come to the end of the Red River?

I wonder if Papa had a job like this in mind when we left home, but didn't tell me. Where will we drift to next?

5. I Travel with Papa and My Brothers Down the Red River Trail

Saturday, September 26, 1846

We camped beside the Pembina trading post today. We'll stay here, Papa says, until the cart train is made up. After all my hard work Papa has sold some of our pemmican to Kittson for a good price, to give us more room on the cart.

The boys and I looked inside the trading post this afternoon. It smelled of new pine logs. I did not expect to see the huge number of things that hung on the walls. Shelves held bolts of cloth in bright colors and patterns. Tiny colored beads, the kind Ojibwe use to trim moccasins, nestled in boxes. A rack held needles, pins, and thread. Spoons and ladles hung on the wall next to frying pans and saucepans. Iron kettles were stacked on the floor, and axes, chains, knives, and guns hung above them.

Near the round black stove in the center, some men were talking. I stood in the back of the store looking at things when Kittson and Jacques, who will lead the cart train, came into the store, followed by Papa. Kittson was talking in a loud voice. He told Papa they hadn't decided which trail the cart train should take.

"The west side of the Red River is the flattest," Jacques said. "There are fewer rivers to ford and almost no trees." Jacques had led some travelers to St. Paul before, but had never taken a long cart train.

"I worry about that side of the river," Kittson said. "Dakota warriors rove along the river. They have attacked cart trains on that side."

Kittson showed a map to Jacques and Papa. "This way, east of the river, is safer, but there are forests and big swamps to cross," Kittson said. Jacques said he had never gone that route.

"Lately the Ojibwe have been friendlier than the Dakota," Kittson said.

Then I heard Papa's voice. "I can speak a little Ojibwe," he said. I smiled to myself because he speaks almost none. I perked up to listen, though, when I heard him say, "My daughter speaks and understands it."

By then Papa had noticed me and nodded in my direction. The men turned to look at me as I stood by the brooms and axes.

"Is that so?" Kittson asked in his booming voice. The room became quiet. They seemed to be waiting for an answer.

"Yes, I can speak Ojibwe," I said. "I learned it from my mother when I was little."

"That's good. What's your name?"

"Josette," I said.

Kittson nodded his head and kept on with his conversation. "It's good you signed on, Dupre," he said to Papa. "Your girl could be helpful on the trail." His finger traced the east route on the map for Papa and Jacques to see. "That decides it then. You'll take the east route. There are trading posts along that way, if the weather turns cold. Plan to leave early Monday."

Thoughts began to whirl in my head as the men continued making plans. I was still angry with Papa for making these decisions without discussing them with me. But if I had to go down the trail, I did want to be useful. It would be me they would depend on to translate if there were any problems during the trip. I wondered if we would meet any Ojibwe or Dakota and if they would be friendly. I was afraid those we meet might pronounce words in a different way than the people in Nokomis's village.

Several men from the buffalo hunt have signed on as trail-cart drivers. Stan and Charlie, who made space for us to park next to them when we arrived at the buffalo hunt, will be drivers. So will Jake, who acts so silly, and Nick. I met them the night we had the dance at the hunt. There may be some others along whose names I never learned, too. I've not forgotten the young man who had a friendly smile for me when we danced at the buffalo hunt. Today I learned his name is Denis, and that he has signed up to be a teamster on the cart train. I have never talked to him, but he seemed nice that night. He is tall, and his eyes crinkle up when he smiles. He has very good manners, and most of the others do not.

Sunday, September 27, 1846

Today I repacked the cart. I put the bags of wild rice and the pemmican in the back because we will eat the food Kittson gave us first and hope to catch game and fish. Papa gave me money to buy other supplies, and I got dried peas and beans, cornmeal and maple syrup. I got just a little salt because Mama hardly ever used it. Most of the time she added dried herbs and maple sugar for seasoning. Then I bought a bag of hard candy. I let each of the boys take a piece and saved the rest to share on the trail. I hung Mama's big kettle and the frying pan with the long handle on the outside of the cart to save space.

"There will not be a driver for every cart," Papa said to me. "Each teamster will be in charge of at least three. Our own cart with our belongings will be first, and you and the boys can ride on that one.

"Two other carts will carry trade goods, furs, and pemmican. The two carts will be tied with ours so that only one driver is needed. The ox will pull the first one, with two horses helping pull the other carts. Kittson said this is a fairly small cart train going to St. Paul. In the spring a larger one will make the trip."

We're leaving first thing tomorrow from Fort Pembina. We're all worried that it will snow before we get to St. Paul. I went to sleep dreading the weeks ahead.

Monday, September 28, 1846

This morning there was a big send-off for everyone leaving on the cart train. Kittson's crew served pancakes, ham, and maple syrup. There were so many people that I couldn't tell who was serving and who was going with us. Kittson introduced Jacques LaRoche as the guide and leader on the trail. He is experienced, Kittson said, and will settle any disputes along the way.

After breakfast we went down to the bank of the Red River, and Papa led the ox pulling our cart onto the raft that they call a ferry. Papa stayed by the ox to be sure it wouldn't get frightened or try to walk off.

It was a sunny day, and breezes blew through our hair as we sat on the cart. We looked down into the watery depths of the Red River passing beneath us. Willow branches with slender green leaves bent low over the water on either side. Sumac bushes had turned the bright red colors of fall. From our lofty place on the wagon, it was a beautiful sight.

"That's our river, isn't it?" Armond called out in his thin, high voice as we floated to the opposite bank.

"Yes, that's true," I said. "If we could go north instead of south, we would get to the forks that go to St. Boniface or to St. Eustache."

On the second ferry, men had to push the other two carts and the horses onto it. There were many to help. I don't suppose it will be this easy to cross rivers on the rest of the trip. At breakfast Jacques had said there might be as many as two hundred streams and rivers to cross between the Red River and the Mississippi.

Once all the carts and animals were across and each teamster had his loads tied together, we followed the other carts south along the river with Jacques in the lead. Once we got started, the shrieks and groans of the carts were so loud, we could hardly hear each other talk. It went so slowly that we walked alongside part of the time. It's hard to believe that this cart will be our home for the next four to six weeks, until we get to St. Paul.

It occurred to me that I could go back to St. Eustache and tell Marguerite and Angelique Nolin that I would work at the school, or in their house, in order to stay with them. They never suggested such an arrangement, but they didn't know how Papa's plans would change. Then I remembered what Mama said the night she died: "Take good care of them, Josette." So I feel I can't leave them, especially Armond, who needs me. If Mama looks down and knows what we're doing or where we're going, I hope that she knows I'm doing my best, even though I am furious at Papa.

Tuesday, September 29, 1846

We stopped for the night in a clearing. Jacques calls this Two Rivers. It was our first chance to see who else is with us. I noticed there was a family with children. When the mother saw me and the boys, she came over to greet us. Her name is Rosalie LaBarre. She and her husband, Vincent, are going to St. Paul to join her husband's brother. She says they've wanted to go there but thought it too risky to travel alone, so she's glad Vincent heard about the cart train, even though it's not really meant for passengers. With Rosalie I'll have someone to chat with. She has a three-year-old named Julie clinging to her skirt. Her boy, Alexander, is the right age for Pierre to play with. Although she seemed like a little girl, eleven-year-old Veronica immediately wanted to do things with me. There is no one Armond's age, so I'll probably have to watch him carefully. But he tries to make friends with everyone.

Pierre and Alexander gathered sticks and branches to build a fire. Pierre was even able to get the fire started with Papa's flint. And I got supper started before we put our bedrolls over the soft-colored, fallen leaves. Others on this cart train seem relieved to be on their way. I'm sad that this trip is taking me away from my school, my teachers, and my dreams of going to school in Montreal—away from nice towns and into the American wilderness!

Wednesday, September 30, 1846

Papa surprised us this morning. He had the fire going when I woke up and had made his own coffee. Water was boiling for me to stir in cornmeal for mush. What we didn't eat, I poured into a pan to harden. When it gets cold, we'll eat slices of it with maple syrup, just like Mama used to feed us.

The teamsters have their own rations, and each does his own cooking, except for Vincent and Papa, who eat with their families. Stan and Charlie, the young men who were parked next to us at the buffalo hunt, are friendly. They had given us game when they caught more than they could eat at the hunt. Some of the men are really boisterous and loud. Jake and Henriot had winked and pinched girls while dancing at the hunt party. When I was writing in my book earlier, Jake came up behind me and scared me by putting his hands over my eyes and shouting, "Surprise!" I was not excited to see him. He thought he was hilarious. It gave me the shivers to have him touch me.

Jacques announced that we will try to make fifteen miles each day. The Tamarack River which we had to cross was fifteen feet wide but only a foot deep. Papa hopped on the cart beside Armond and Pierre, and rode across as the ox went right through the water. I always sit behind them on a sack so I can see above the sides. I pull out my journal when we're going slow or resting. If I can't write in the journal during the day, then I try to write when we stop for the night.

After the crossing we found a nice camping spot. Jacques said it's a rule of the trail to cross the river before we make camp whenever we can.

The children gathered wood tonight while Papa and Vincent caught fish. Rosalie and Vincent started the fire and invited us to use it, too. After we put away the pots and dishes, Rosalie and I talked. She is going to have a baby this winter. She said she is looking forward to living in a new place. I'm not, but I didn't speak my mind, because I don't know her very well yet. I still feel we are going in the wrong direction, away from everyone we have ever known. I wish I could speak more openly to Papa about this; but we are surrounded by people all the time, and he would shush me by saying I'm being disrespectful.

I decided to read a story to the children from the book Marguerite Nolin gave me. When I looked up, I saw Denis sitting across the fire, watching me as I read to them.

We drifted into sleep on beds we rolled out on the ground to the chirping and croaking of millions of frogs. They made me feel as if we were alone in a world of strange talking creatures.

Thursday, October 1, 1846

Papa was up early again today, anxious to get started.

"It's already October," he reminded everyone. Papa worries because we have such a long way to go, even though Kittson told him fall and spring are the best times to make this trip.

At night we had a bad thunderstorm. Lightning crackled when it lit up the sky, and I could see the carts, horses, and oxen in bright light. It felt as if the storm were right on top of us. Even Papa seemed scared. We moved our blankets under the wagon, and the boys covered their heads. Armond hung on to me as though I could save him. I was afraid, too, but I didn't want to miss seeing the storm. It seems much more powerful than when you see it from inside a house. The rain settled down to a steady soaking that lasted most of the night.

Friday, October 2, 1846

Our things got soaked last night. All our clothes were wet, but we had to wear them anyway. I hate their itchy, moist feeling. They still hadn't dried out by the afternoon, and it made me grumpy.

"You have to get used to it, Josette," Papa said when I complained. "When I was a voyageur, this happened many times." I just wish Papa would feel a little sympathy for me and the boys. Now there are giant black horseflies flying around that light on our sticky skin. We've all got itchy bites. When Pierre and Armond whine to me, I tell them to speak to Papa.

Tonight when we stopped, we could see gravel ridges alongside the trail. Veronica and I took Armond and walked over to them, hoping the wind would dry out our damp clothes. The ridges were as high as small mountains. We were stepping through the tall grass trying to reach them when suddenly a whole flock of prairie chickens flew up right in our faces and startled us completely. Veronica and Armond screamed. I didn't know what was happening at first. There was a huge shushing sound as they rose up into the air. The poor things were probably just as startled as we were. I had to carry Armond all the way back. Now, lying here on the ground, I can still feel those chicken feathers flapping against my face.

Armond started coughing yesterday, and now Pierre is feeling feverish. I think they'll both have colds by tomorrow. I wish Papa seemed more concerned, but he's used to leaving that to Mama.

Today the trail crossed the Snake and Middle rivers. Jacques says it's halfway between Pembina and the Red Lake River. He walks back from his place at the front each day and shows the map to Papa. He said he wants me to look at it, too, so that I know where we are and am prepared if we meet any Ojibwe along the way.

Veronica follows me around whenever we're camped. I don't mind her company as much as I thought

I would. It's better not to be alone, because sometimes the men tease me. Jake sneaked up behind me again when I was stirring the supper stew and dropped something down the back of my dress.

"Scared ya, didn't I!" he said with a cackling laugh. I got Veronica to help me find what he put down my dress, and she pulled out a horrible dead bird. I glowered at Jake while he looked at me with a toothless grin. Finally he went back to his carts. The other teamsters just laughed. I'm the only young person on this trip who isn't still a child. The men think it's all right to tease me. Sometimes I feel they get too familiar. Some of them are nice, though, and I don't think I'd mind getting to know them.

Then I looked up and again saw that Denis was sitting on a log across the fire from me, watching the whole scene. I was embarrassed. I wasn't acting very ladylike or mature like the Nolin sisters had taught us.

Sunday, October 4, 1846

There's been a change of weather. Dry autumn grass rustles beneath our feet, and hot winds have turned our faces red. The children are sicker today. I thought it was a cold, but they are hot and feverish. Rosalie is worried that it could be scarlatina. I'm worried, too. Rosalie says she and Veronica had it several years ago. People don't usually get it a second time, she told me. Even Papa says he feels like he's coming down with something.

It was a long way down to the Red Lake River, where we camped for the night. Jacques said the trees here are oak, poplar, elm, and ironwood. He knows so much about trees and plants! We filled our jugs from a spring of clear water that flowed over the rocks. The grass was thick, and Papa and Pierre put the ox and horses out to pasture. At bedtime on most nights, crickets chirp steadily and crows land nearby. The birds' big black presence is never menacing. It makes me think of Nokomis and her crow stories.

I am worried about the fever that so many are getting. We must have caught this illness at the buffalo hunt with so many people from different places coming together.

Compared to being at the hunt, this has actually been a pleasant journey. Of course, I wish I was back in school more than anything. But the weather has been good, we find water whenever we need it, and the hunting and fishing has given us fresh food along the wooded way.

Jacques brought his wrinkled map back to our cart

tonight to show Papa and me. Small rivers were not drawn on it. It showed the Red River with Pembina at the top, the Mississippi River starting in the north, and St. Paul at the bottom. There was a lot of open space, but no marked paths. He thought not many carts had taken this trail before. So far I have not been fearful about finding our way. I'm only worried that the boys still have a fever.

After we stopped, Jacques gathered the whole group together. He warned us that Dakota and Ojibwe are common in this area. The teamsters must stay in camp unless they tell Jacques where they are going.

"Do not fire guns," Jacques said. "Shots attract attention. This rule is laid down for your protection."

I wonder if or when we'll meet others on this trail. I hope we won't come across a war party. Will I need to translate any Ojibwe before we get to St. Paul? I hope so, but not if the men are hostile.

At suppertime we couldn't find Pierre or Alexander. They like to sneak off so Armond doesn't beg to go along. They had been warned by Papa and Vincent about going off exploring when we stopped for the night, so we were all annoyed. We weren't worried at first, but when they didn't come when we called them for dinner, we ate quickly and began to search in earnest.

There were gunshots in the distance. Alarmed, the men searched farther from the camp. Rosalie and I watched the younger children by our fire.

"Maybe they've gone to the river to fish," Rosalie said when the men returned.

"I'll head back over that way," Vincent said as he stood up, but I knew Papa had already looked there. Finally Jacques came by, and Papa had to tell him the boys were gone.

"Henriot's gone, too," Jacques said. "He likes to take off on his own."

Jacques offered to help Papa look for the boys. They were about to leave when an Ojibwe hunting party came out of the woods. They didn't respond when Jacques called out to them. Papa left to search for the boys, but Jacques decided to stay in camp, since the Ojibwe were there. The hunting party would not speak to Jacques. Instead they started to rummage through the carts. When they lifted the covering on our cart, I spoke.

"*Boozhoo*," I called out in Ojibwe. "Boozhoo," I repeated in a louder voice. When they didn't respond, I tried some of the words Adele had taught me in Dakota. They turned from the carts and looked at me.

I spoke haltingly in Dakota and in English. "*Wan-*

yaka wasicun—seen white man? *Mazak an bosdoka*—shoot off a gun? *Akita hoksiidan*—seek boy."

"Boozhoo," they said, which wasn't really an answer, but they left the cart alone. I asked them again in Ojibwe if they had heard gunshots, and they nodded. Then I decided they were Ojibwe and told them that the gunshots had not come from our camp.

"We have been looking for two young boys from our camp who went exploring," I said, and they could understand me.

"We're worried about the gunshots we heard because we've just been told that one of our party might have gone out hunting by himself," I went on. One of them came closer, much closer, to me and started to ask questions in a friendly way. He wanted to know who I was and where I came from. He was curious about the Ojibwe I knew, which was a little different from his. He wondered how I knew Dakota words, too. Finally he came out with the question that he was most curious about.

"Are you a prisoner of these people?" he asked, because I look Ojibwe.

By now some of the teamsters had come over to listen. Our visitors looked suspiciously at the dirty, rough-looking teamsters.

I smiled at that and told him no, that I was traveling with Papa. Feverish little Armond must have thought he was threatening me because he ran to me and hugged me around my legs. I told him we were just passing through on our way south and would leave in the morning. I'm not sure he believed me. I think he had hoped I would say I was being held against my will so he could rescue me. He explained that he thought I might be a Dakota girl who had been taken in a raid.

Jacques approached them with pemmican and a fish he had caught that morning. The men left as quickly as they came after that. I spent the next hour worrying because it was getting dark and Papa hadn't come back. Armond and I went down to the river to fill our water jug. Just then Henriot came walking along the bank with Alexander and Pierre, who still had his arm in a sling. I started yelling at the boys and told them they had missed their supper. Before I could say more, Henriot started defending himself.

"I wanted to do a little hunting," he said, "and thought that if I went far enough away, no one would hear the shots. The boys must have followed me."

Just then Papa came back. Vincent had already re-turned. Vincent and Papa looked at Pierre and Alexander grimly. Henriot protested that he thought he'd bring back some game, but Jacques was angry.

"If the Ojibwe thought you were shooting at them, they could have attacked and killed us all," Jacques warned. "It doesn't matter if you got anything. It is shooting that lets others in the woods know we are here."

"You are not to go off with Henriot again," Papa said sternly to Pierre. Papa and Vincent took Pierre and Alexander to the edge of the camp and gave them a good thrashing. Papa doesn't usually do that; but Vincent does, and he thought each boy should be treated alike. The boys crawled into their bedrolls without supper.

I think Henriot acted as childishly as the boys. When everybody quieted down, I crawled over to Pierre in the darkness and handed him a piece of bread. He said he wasn't hungry, and I could see that he had been crying. I felt his forehead and realized he still had a slight fever.

"Papa was so worried," I said. "I wonder what we would have done if we couldn't find you. Now that we know that Ojibwe are near, Papa and Jacques don't want to stay in this area another day."

"We didn't mean to scare you; we just wanted to explore," Pierre said in a shaky voice. "I wish we were back in St. Eustache with our old friends."

"So do I," I said to him, but I felt guilty. I wondered whose side I should be taking. Even though the boys had disobeyed, I gave Pierre a hug and kissed him good night before I crept back to my own bedroll.

6. Denis Follows the Cart Train After It Divides

Monday, October 5, 1846

We have had a change of plans. Papa and Jacques have divided the cart train into two groups to separate us from the teamsters. I think that Henriot taking the boys out hunting had a lot to do with this decision.

Papa, Vincent, and their two families will stay together toward the back of the train. Jacques has arranged for Denis to bring up the rear as a lookout for warriors or wild animals that could be following us. I'm excited because I might get to talk to him sometimes. Of all the teamsters he seems the quietest and the nicest. He will have the last string of carts and be with our group for most meals. Anyway, I'll feel better near Denis, Vincent, and Papa, away from the other teamsters at the front of the train. Papa says some of the other teamsters are just trying to be friendly, but he doesn't realize how creepy their looks seem to me.

Rosalie and I told Denis that we would cook for him from now on because he will be the last to come into camp. Today Veronica rode with us, and Pierre sat on Rosalie's cart with Alexander. Veronica chatters all the time, which makes the time go more quickly.

Rosalie had fun planning a special meal tonight in honor of Denis. Denis enticed three grouse into a snare he made with kernels of corn. Rosalie told Denis that he was resourceful. He handed the birds to her as though they were a prize.

We made a cobbler using the saskatoon berries I had picked along with some dry blueberries that Rosalie had brought. I would have liked a dandelion salad, but the greens are too bitter this time of year.

All night we heard the coyotes' lonely howls. I was glad they were on the other side of the river. The stream runs full below the willows where we're camped.

Tuesday, October 6, 1846

This morning Jacques and Papa paced the bank of the Red Lake River, trying to decide how to cross it. The river was too deep to ford. Jacques decided we must empty the carts and take off the wheels. Some teamsters groaned and whispered, but Papa, Denis, and Vincent agreed it was best. We unloaded each cart and took the wheels off. Then the men laid poles on top of the cart frames and rested the wheels on top. We piled the goods on top of the wheels. One man entered the water on each side of a wheelless cart to keep the load from tipping as the cart floated in the current. I lay facedown on top of our cart with my arm over Pierre on one side and Armond on the other. Our horses and oxen pulled us through as they swam to the other side. Papa waded through the water, guiding the floating wagon.

All of a sudden there was a sudden lurch, like the bottom of the cart hit something, and Pierre got up on his hands and knees. I couldn't hold him down. He slipped off the side and into the water. Thankfully, Denis was just behind, guiding Papa's second cart, and he scooped Pierre out of the water and threw him up on the opposite bank.

"I wanted to see what was happening," Pierre protested, "and I rolled off. Now I'm all wet," he complained. Armond hung on to me for dear life and wouldn't let go when I got off the cart. He's getting too big and heavy to be such a big baby.

We were all thankful as well as exhausted when the river crossing was finally over. It took all day. I talked with Jacques tonight for a while, and he confessed he was also unnerved by the crossing today. Since he has never married and his parents are dead, he hopes that if anybody dies on this trip, it will be him. He admitted that this journey is more hazardous than he had expected. He feels the weight of the responsibility of getting us all the way to St. Paul. I think I understand how he feels. I urged him to sleep well tonight.

Wednesday, October 7, 1846

During the river crossing many things got damp, or splashed on, even if they were floating above the water most of the time yesterday. Rosalie and I laughed about our dresses. I found a deerskin dress of Mama's to wear until my cotton one dries out.

This afternoon we went through a strange, silent area. A fire had passed through ahead of us. Black trees, bushes, and grass were everywhere. Charred trees stood black and lifeless, pointing their skeletons to the sky. The air seemed heavy and lifeless. No animals could be seen, except for some enormous gray cranes stalking majestically through a swamp. It was like this the whole way between Turtle Creek and the Sand Hill River. Even the tops of the swamp grasses were scorched.

A feeling of aloneness has come over me. It feels as though no other people have ever wandered this way, except for our solitary band of travelers. We came to a clearing where there were sandhills several hundred feet high. We camped there on the sandy ground.

Papa and I avoid speaking to each other.

Friday, October 9, 1846

Jacques didn't know which way to go this morning. The trail has disappeared among the burned trees and sandhills. He got out his map but still wasn't sure. He directed the carts southeast, according to the sun, and hoped it was right. Even though I've never gone down the trail before, it seems to reassure him to talk it over with me. This makes me feel good.

This afternoon we came to another stream. It didn't look deep, so I thought I might as well wade across with Armond. My foot slipped on the muddy bank, and I fell into the water and felt as if I was being sucked under. Papa was ahead, leading his train of carts and didn't see me. Before I knew what was happening, Denis jumped into the water, reached down, and pulled me up.

"Don't be afraid. I've got Armond," he said into my ear. Armond clung to him. I was getting my footing when Denis put his other arm around my waist and half lifted me across. Denis's arm felt steady and strong. I wasn't really afraid of drowning because it wasn't very deep. I was embarrassed, though, because I knew I looked like a drowned chicken. It was lucky my shoes were on the cart.

While we made supper I tried to dry off near the fire. Then I ran a little by the river, but it didn't help much. After we ate, we sat around the fire. Denis sat down next to me to ask how I was. I told him I felt fine. He stayed there until Armond tried to squeeze between us.

"Just a minute, little man," Denis said. "There's room on either side of us." I blushed at that. I thanked him for saving us and prompted Armond to do so, too. Armond kept asking for a story until I read a short one. Denis watched the pages the whole time. As I went to sleep my mind kept reliving that little scene again and again.

The other teamsters came down to our fire after they had eaten and began to tease Jacques.

"How many more surprises do you have up your

sleeve?" they asked. He tried to defend himself by laughing it off.

"I never know how deep a river will be," said Jacques. "We're all still here. Our goods on the carts are still with us. That was what I was charged to do. So far, so good."

I can see why Kittson chose him. He does a good job of keeping everyone satisfied. I still keep my distance from Papa but find this trip bearable, even interesting, because of Jacques and Denis.

Saturday, October 10, 1846

Today we entered a forest of large trees with moss-covered trunks and camped among the Detroit Lakes.

We expected to meet more Ojibwe along the way, but have not seen any yet. Since crossing the Red River on the first day of our journey, we have not seen any other humans except the three Ojibwe men in the hunting party.

Tuesday, October 13, 1846

It has been cold and rainy the past two days as we traveled east toward the Leaf Mountains. Every brook is now a river, every bog a lake, and even the trail itself has become a swamp! Cold steam rises from the soaked earth. Our spirits are dampened, too.

Papa took a chill when we were crossing the Red Lake River, and since then has been coughing and wheezing. He stayed on the cart, huddled under his heavy jacket, instead of joking with the other cart drivers. Mama knew how to make him feel better when he came back from his trips as a voyageur. He'd often be hoarse from singing all day. He'd let Mama treat him with any remedy she wanted to try.

Papa says that there's nothing to worry about, but I'm scared. We need Papa, despite how I sometimes feel about him. If he got really sick, what would we do? Papa's sickness could turn into something like consumption. How could I take care of him and the boys, and drive the cart? Pierre couldn't even help drive the cart with his sling. Papa could even die. Then we would be orphans.

This afternoon I said that if Papa were to lie down on the cart for a while, I could hold the reins. Most of the time it's not difficult. The animals just follow one another on the trail. Jacques is at the front, deciding where the first cart will go.

We've been traveling only about two weeks, but already it seems like forever. I think this trip is exhausting

Rosalie, though she will not admit it. Her baby is not coming until after Christmas, so she doesn't worry, because we'll be in St. Paul before that. But that worries me, too. What if the baby is born early, and she gets sick like Mama did? Who is there to care for her family but me? Sometimes I feel I don't have enough time to think about all the things that could go wrong.

Unlike me, Rosalie is always in a merry mood and cheers up all of us. She pokes fun at herself or her family to keep us amused. When Armond won't smile, she teases him until the corners of his mouth turn up.

Thursday, October 15, 1846

We left the flatlands some time ago. Now we're going through hilly country. As our carts go down one hill the carts ahead of us disappear over the next one. Pierre and Alexander are tired of sitting on our bumpy cart. Since fording the last stream two days ago, they have walked alongside. They run up to other carts, play tag with the driver, and then fall back to us. Lately, they have taken to running ahead of our caravan, and racing down the hills ahead of the carts. I don't think it is safe. The carts go much faster downhill, and the teamsters can't always hold the horses and oxen back. Pierre and Alexander are having so much fun, they don't listen to me. By the end of the afternoon, all the teamsters were yelling, "Boys, get out of our way."

I have taken over the reins quite a bit lately, and I've found that it is not hard. Jacques says that after we make three fords of the Ottertail River tomorrow, we will reach a trading post. I decided we should all have a treat. I've been doling out the candy I bought in Pembina carefully. Lately, I've wanted to save most of it for Papa's coughing spells. When I opened the bag today, I was shocked to see that there were only two pieces left.

"Pierre, the candy bag is almost empty!" I said in consternation. I turned to look at him, but he looked straight ahead and didn't answer. Now that I've been driving part of the time, I can't watch what goes on behind me. "Pierre," I repeated, "we have to save what's left for Papa when he's coughing."

Papa was dozing. He didn't understand what was happening, and when he lifted his head, he said, "Children, stop quarreling." He closed his eyes again. I have been trying my best, but Papa doesn't notice. Pierre jumped off our cart the first chance he had and has been riding with Alexander ever since.

I sat on the wagon holding the reins and watching the rears of the animals as they plodded on heavily. What a relief to stop at night and get a fire going! It's a good thing we keep a little dry kindling on the cart to get it started.

Today the teamsters ahead called out that axles on two carts had snapped. The entire train had to stop. To fix them, the broken carts had to be unloaded, trees cut down, and the trunks fashioned into new axles. Vincent and Denis went up ahead to help. Papa went, too, even though everyone told him to save his strength. It took a while to find two trees the right size that were straight and cut them down. Then the logs had to be fashioned at each end to fit the center holes of the wheels. Rosalie and I sat on the carts for a while, but finally I walked up front to watch the progress.

As the hours went by, Rosalie and I talked to Jacques about camping for the night instead of going on. We built a fire and put on a boiling pot of stew, made with pemmican and vegetables, for the whole crew. It was ready when the men's work was done. This is the first time we've all eaten together since Papa and Jacques separated the families from the teamster crew. I overheard one teamster say this was the last time he would go on a train that had children along. Everyone was tired out by the time we were finished. We all curled up in our blankets early.

Tonight I heard Papa coughing a lot. I'll be worried if this hangs on because it reminds me of the time Mama got her fever. It's hard to keep feeling mean toward Papa when he's feeling so poorly and we need him so much.

Friday, October 16, 1846

Today was one of the worst days on the journey. This morning we headed toward the Crow Wing crossing. Jacques thought the teamsters should take the wheels off the carts and float them across, as they did before. The drivers up ahead complained because it is a lot of extra work. They wanted to wade in the water and guide the loads across. Jacques gave in and let the drivers try it. Papa still has got a bad cough, but he insisted on wading into the river. The drivers had to hold the carts back at the steep banks.

One of the teamsters, Augustin, was driving the carts just ahead of us. I saw him walking down the bank next to his horses when he slipped and slid down into the water. He didn't say a word—he just disappeared. The heavy cart rolled down right behind him. It happened right before our eyes. Other teamsters pulled Augustin out as soon as they could reach him.

After we got across, Rosalie and I tried to revive Augustin. He hadn't been under the water long, but he was very muddy and bloody when they pulled him up on the other shore! I wished Adele were here. I surely wished Nokomis had given me some lessons on caring for people who are sick or injured. She knew something to try for every sickness. I feel so helpless. Rosalie said she thought Augustin's internal parts must have been crushed under the wheels. Jacques tried to bleed him, but no one was trained to do anything else.

In the evening everyone was quiet, except for an occasional cough from Papa. The boys didn't tease or jump around. We laid out cold food and ate close to the fire. I sat by Augustin until I heard him stop breathing. I had hardly ever talked to him, but I felt I had lost a friend.

During the evening Jacques assigned the three carts Augustin's team was pulling to other teamsters. That means that three drivers will have an extra cart, but Jacques gave them the extra animals to use as well.

"I let the teamsters talk me out of crossing the safe way," Jacques said at the end of the evening. He put his head in his hands as we sat by the fire, and I reached over and patted his leg. I'm sorry he is so discouraged.

Sunday, October 18, 1846

Before daybreak the teamsters dug a grave just off the trail and buried Augustin. I hated to leave him there and wondered when anyone will ever pass this way again. I knew we had to move on because the days are getting much colder. The drivers were very somber as we began today, because they knew that Augustin's accident could have happened to any one of them. As we were leaving, Jacques stopped the cart train at the spot where they buried Augustin. I knelt by the grave and most of the others did, too, to say a prayer for him. Even the bravest men had tears in their eyes as they climbed back on their loads. What a cold, dreary journey this is getting to be.

Tuesday, October 20, 1846

We're headed east toward the Mississippi River now. We have had rain this past week and often got mired in bogs. The teamsters steadied each load to prevent it from tipping while others pushed the carts. The boys and I walked most of the time because the carts are already hard enough to push. One time we became stuck, and as we jumped off the cart the boys pushed me, trying to get off first. My precious journal fell into the mud. I was furious. The back cover got muddy, but the pages inside weren't ruined. I shouted at Pierre, "Be more careful! This book came from France, you know."

There were several fallen trees on the trail today, and Denis went to the front of the train to help. Even though the weather is cool, he took off his jacket. I couldn't help but watch his muscles moving under his shirt when he swung the ax. He glanced up, saw that I was watching, and sent me a beaming smile. I looked down because I felt warm all over and knew my face must be pink.

Every time the men heave a tree to the side, they call out until the woods ring with their shouting. These sounds make the forest come alive. The teamsters even seem to be having fun! Papa tries to work like a young man. I don't know why his cough is hanging on so long, but it seems to me he coughs more when he smokes his clay pipe. He says he's getting better, but I'm not sure. Armond's nose runs all the time in this windy, cold weather, and he hates to have me wipe it. He doesn't have a fever anymore, so I'm not worried, but I hope his sniffles are over soon. He likes to sit on my lap so I can wrap Mama's coat around both of us and keep us warmer.

This afternoon the teamsters were in dismay over the soft, muddy ground. Rosalie suggested they cut branches off fir trees and lay them on the path. Most of the men didn't think it would work, but they didn't have any better ideas! It took hours to cut the branches. Rosalie and I dragged them to the muddiest part of the trail with the help of the children. The pine-scented branches tickled our faces as we carried them. The carts rolled more easily over the branches. We felt good because they listened to us. Rosalie even got some praise from some of the teamsters.

Thursday, October 22, 1846

The air was nippy this morning, and the bright yellow leaves left on the trees stood out against the blue sky. By the afternoon the sky had became dark gray, the wind came up, and it started to snow. Big flakes whirled across the path and brushed across our faces. The snow did not last long, but fear clutched my heart. We could all be lost if a real snowstorm were to overtake us.

"I hope Kittson knew what he was doing, having us start this late in the season," Papa said. Denis was eating with us, and he said he hoped so, too, but that one thing nobody can really depend on is the weather being the same from one year to another. We've been away from other people for so many days that it feels like we could be forgotten and die here alone in the snow.

Saturday, October 24, 1846

Today we finally arrived at the Mississippi River. We had been traveling along the bank of the Crow Wing River where it joined a wide stream. When Jacques told the teamsters up front that the stream must be the western shore of the Mississippi River, they let out a yell. The shouts passed from one cart to another. We've heard so much about this famous river that I thought it would be much wider than it is. Still, it is a beautiful river.

"We no longer have to worry about losing the trail," Jacques said as he got out his clay pipe and tobacco pouch, and stretched out under a tree. "We can just follow the river all the way to St. Paul."

Pierre and Armond ran to the edge of the riverbank to look, then Papa warned them of the danger.

"Be careful, boys! We don't need any more accidents," he said. When we left home, I felt that I was leaving civilization behind, along with my school, church, home, and Papa's family in St. Boniface. Now I feel a little bit better. We are closer to our destination, and our family has not yet had a bad mishap. Papa seems very pleased with the way things are going, but I'm still not so sure. We really don't know what we'll find in St. Paul.

Sunday, October 25, 1846

As we camped by the river last night Jacques and the teamsters discussed the best way to cross it. Men from a small village of Ojibwe approached as they were talking. Jacques motioned to me, and we went to greet them. They were very friendly.

"We have our village here so that we can help travelers cross the river," the leader said. They looked at the number of carts and dickered with Jacques about the fee they wanted to take us across. We were surprised to discover that they speak Ojibwe, some French, and even a little English. They helped pull the loads down the bank, knew the best place to navigate the icy water, and helped guide the carts up on the other side. It took a long time, but the teamsters had an easy time of it because of their help. Papa claims to be feeling better and is eager to keep going.

"We'll soon be there," Papa told the boys when we crossed the river.

I wish we had a better map of our journey. The one Jacques has doesn't help much. He showed me where he thinks we crossed the Mississippi. It's strange, but now Jacques often consults with me about the direction we should take. I feel partly responsible for getting us all down the trail safely. I even think Papa is proud that I have been useful, even though he never says so to me. When we get to St. Paul, Papa will have completed his obligations to Kittson.

Tuesday, October 27, 1846

Tonight we stopped at Aitken's Trading Post. A big man with a bushy black beard, named Alan Morrison, had a warm, friendly greeting for each of us.

"Welcome to Aitken's Post!" he said, inviting us inside. We clustered around a blazing fire and looked about at the well-stocked shelves. They held goods of every kind, many more of each item than were at the post in Pembina. He called his two daughters from the kitchen.

When the door opened, inviting smells of roast pork and baking bread escaped into the room.

"Marguerite, Mary Ann, there is someone here you'll want to meet." He said to Papa, "It isn't often that children or young women come down the trail. We're glad you made it this far."

Mary Ann was about my age and immediately started to show me around the store. Armond tagged along. Mary Ann said Marguerite helps in the kitchen, but she doesn't have to help until it is time to serve the food. Her mother and sister do the cooking. She took me into the kitchen so I could meet their mother. She is an Ojibwe from the Red River, so the girls are Métis like me. It felt so good, so homey to be in a warm and friendly kitchen. Tears came to my eyes, though, because I will never be in a kitchen with Mama again.

That evening the food was hot, and there was plenty of it; but the best part was being able to eat at a real table instead of cooking over fires and sitting on the ground. Marguerite and Mary Ann chatted and teased the men in a lighthearted manner all during the evening. Some of the teamsters acted silly and loud, but Mary Ann just walked away, laughing at them over her shoulder. Although I think she is a coquette, I wish I could act more like that. I noticed Denis smiling and nodding his head as she talked to him. When she whispered a joke in his ear, he laughed out loud.

After we finished eating, Denis went outside with Marguerite for a walk around the property. I hope he doesn't like her too much. I enjoyed talking with Mary Ann while we washed and put away dishes. I couldn't help watching the door for Denis and Marguerite to return.

Mary Ann told me that they don't go to school anymore because there isn't a teacher near here. She said she doesn't care, because she wants to get married. She hopes one of these days somebody who comes down the trail on the way to St. Paul will be the one for her. I confided in her about my dream of going to school in Montreal. And then I said I even have a dream of going to France someday. I don't know why I said that. I think it was because even though I'll probably never see her again, I wanted her to know I have big dreams.

Seeing Mary Ann's mother busy in the kitchen reminded me of Mama. I wonder if those girls appreciate having their mother with them all the time. Somehow I doubt if they even think about it at all.

How I wish we could live near a family like the Morrisons. In just one night I felt like the girls were my friends.

At bedtime our family went upstairs and made our beds on the floor. It was a luxury to have a roof over our heads. It felt good to snuggle under the covers in a warm, dry place for a night. I felt a little sorry for the teamsters who had to sleep with their carts. Papa said he can feel his head clearing and his cold getting better already.

Wednesday, October 28, 1846

Now that we're on the east bank of the river, the carts follow a level road through sandy hills covered with scrubby grass. We are beginning to see houses.

At the hotel and trading post where we stopped today, we ate wild duck, potatoes, and apple pie. What a change from our tiresome trail diet! Delicious meals two times this week. I hope it is an omen of good things to come. We are all so relieved that we are almost there.

Jacques pointed out homes, inns, and homesteads as we followed the river. We encounter people along the trail every day now.

Saturday, October 31, 1846

I got up before sunrise today to make breakfast. We're almost out of the food that Kittson sent along for the trail. I don't want to dip into our supply of wild rice and pemmican any more than I have to. I know that Jacques must have some money to spend for the teamsters' provisions, but I don't have any idea how much. We passed the Elk River and the Coon Rapids. I can hardly wait to see what we'll find when we get to St. Paul. I imagine it will be a big place with buildings nicer than Fort Garry.

Monday, November 2, 1846

There was a raw, cold wind this morning. Ice appeared on all the ponds, but it melted by noon. This afternoon we crossed the Rum River, so we knew that we were near the Falls of St. Anthony.

Rosalie, Veronica, and I jumped off the carts to look when we heard the loud rushing sound of the water. Soon all the teamsters were gaping as the water crashed over the falls and dropped in a big crescendo to the river below. Jacques said this is a famous landmark. I've heard about these falls for a long time. I expected them to be much bigger and higher. The boys were eager to run down the bank to the river, but we shouted at them to stay near us. We rested on the bank for a while, and Jacques said that much more water passes over the falls in the spring than now. I guess we'll have to come back another time to see that.

Tuesday, November 3, 1846

We stopped at a tavern for the night and had a dry place to sleep. Papa thought it was too expensive, but Jacques said he hadn't used much of the money Kittson gave him to use for the trip, so he paid for the whole group.

Tonight Rosalie and Vincent's family sat with us a long time after we finished eating. Denis stayed, too, rather than sitting with the other teamsters. Papa kept everyone laughing with his funny stories. Of course I've heard them all before. There won't be many more times like this before we reach St. Paul. I never thought I could write that I was sorry that the trip was coming to an end, but I will miss the good times like this. I certainly look forward to a bed of my own and shops where one can buy things one needs.

Wednesday, November 4, 1846

Today we straggled into the town of St. Anthony, on the east side of the Mississippi. Here several routes from Pembina have merged, so we see many travelers now. When we stopped for a rest, a woman told me that Red River carts pass almost every day. She said she does not want such coarse men in her house and will not serve them if they ask for food. Standing beside her, I realized that our cart train must look like a very motley bunch of travelers to people as we pass.

Thursday, November 5, 1846

The Mississippi is much wider now, as it has been joined by the St. Peters from the west. We are camping at an unfinished trading post called the Halfway House between St. Anthony and St. Paul. It is unheated, but at least we are off the ground. It will be so good when we find a comfortable place in St. Paul with real beds. I fell asleep thinking about finally getting to St. Paul, where we will stay over the winter. Then I dreamed of our cozy home in St. Eustache; but when I woke up, it was getting light, and we were all cold.

Friday, November 6, 1846

This morning we cut across the Territorial Road through a place Jacques called Prospect Park. We followed along the road from St. Anthony to St. Paul even after nightfall. Our carts finally screeched to a halt at the river's edge. We camped there, just like any other night on the trail. I would never have guessed it was St. Paul if Jacques hadn't told me. There were no lights anywhere, so we couldn't see the town. The boys had fallen asleep and didn't even know we had reached our destination.

The quiet sound of the mighty river flowing beside us gave me hope that we had come to a good place.

7. I Cried When I Saw St. Paul

Saturday, November 7, 1846

When I opened my eyes this morning, I was so disappointed, I cried. All I could see were a few shabby, unpainted wood buildings clustered around a boat landing where the cart train was tied up. Across from the landing, a sign on a building read Jackson's Store. On both sides of the landing were high rock cliffs that hung out almost over the flat place that was the boat landing.

There was no snow, the trees had lost their leaves, and everything looked gray. It was dreadful to think that we left home for this place. Papa must know that he has made a horrible mistake.

Pierre and Armond woke up this morning as Papa got up. "Look. We're in St. Paul, boys," he said. I thought maybe he was trying to be cheerful for the benefit of me and the boys. The boys lifted their heads. They were not excited, and Armond just put his head down again.

Jacques had a meeting and told all the teamsters that they and their loads must wait together until a steamboat comes for the goods. Nobody knows what day that will be, but the boat has to be loaded to leave before the river freezes. It doesn't freeze early here, but a wide spot downriver called Lake Pepin usually freezes over in November. The men must stay with their loads at all times. They take turns eating and sleeping.

While Papa was at the meeting I took the boys with me to look around a bit. It was a dark, cloudy day, and the breeze had a little bite to it. I had hoped that when we arrived, it would be a sunshiny day. At least that would be something to be cheery about. We walked over to the river's edge. It is the widest river I have ever seen.

"Come, boys, let's see what else there is to see on a Saturday morning," I said. I looked up at the Jackson's Store sign.

"Let's go inside," I said. "We can stay warm in there." We walked in through a homemade door and found a store just a little bigger than the trading post in Pembina. That was astonishing to me. I had expected a town with stores at least as big as St. Boniface's, probably bigger. Still, the store had most anything anyone could buy on the frontier, from dried beans to fishing tackle, from shovels to bolts of cloth. There were overalls for men, and even ready-made jackets. At the foot of a staircase was a sign with an arrow pointing upward that said ROOMS. In one corner by the stove was a bar for dispensing rum and liquor.

When we warmed up and went back outside, we ran into Denis. I told him I thought we had come to a very dreary place. Denis tried to look on the bright side.

"It feels mighty good to be here and take a rest from driving the carts," he said.

We stood in the cold and agreed that the weather was just as bad as it was at home.

"I'd like to ask you a question," he said.

"What?" I said, trying to think what it could be.

"You enjoy reading to the boys so much. If we have a few days here, could you teach me to read?"

"You don't know how to read?" I knew many of the teamsters had never been to school, but I never expected Denis to say that.

"It's a long story. Please don't tell the others. I don't know how long it will be before we start the long trip back. I was hoping you could help me," Denis said.

"Of course I'll try to help," I said. "But can't you stay here?"

"I don't think so. I signed a contract to go both ways."

My body stiffened when I heard that. I felt betrayed by Papa. How dare Papa keep us here when we could go back home! If we went back this next week, I could go to school for half a year at least.

Before I said more, Denis said, "Your father doesn't want to take you and your brothers back in the wintertime, but Jacques is going to lead us other teamsters back after we unload."

When Papa came back to the carts, I said accusingly, "What else are you keeping from me? I found out Jacques and the other teamsters are going right back to the Red River. We could have gone back now, if you had wanted to. You know how I feel about school."

"You've learned more on this trip than you would have ever learned in a school classroom," Papa said.

But even though I was furious, I was also a little relieved. I couldn't stand thinking about a trip back with the boys right away, not in the winter.

Sunday, November 8, 1846

We wait and wait by the landing and sleep on top or under the loaded carts. The carts are crowded together, and everything stinks. On the trail we moved the animals away from the carts at night. Here animals and their manure are right next to us. Steam rises from both in this cold weather. I can't stand this any longer.

Since my outburst Papa won't talk to me. I don't know where we are going to stay this winter. Papa hasn't bothered to tell me. The boys and I go into Jackson's Store as much as we dare, to get warm, even though there is a sign that says NO LOITERING. Each day I try to buy something, like oatmeal or dried beans. It's a good thing that I put Mama's coat in the cart when we packed because I need it here. I put Pierre's old jacket on Armond to keep him from getting too cold. Pierre wrapped a blanket around his shoulders to keep from shivering, but he really needs a jacket.

At last Papa sent us to Jackson's Store so Pierre could try on jackets. Pierre found one he liked, but I could see that he would grow out of it soon. Instead we bought one that's quite large. In my poor English I told Mrs. Jackson that we would pay for it when Papa gets paid. Mrs. Jackson said he should wear it now to stay warm. I think Papa will say that Pierre made a good choice.

The teamsters will get paid as soon as they can unload the carts. I suppose that's when Papa plans to find a place for the winter. I think he should start looking now.

Vincent's brother came down to the landing to get Rosalie and Vincent and the children this afternoon.

"As soon as I know where his place is, I'll let you know," Rosalie said, and gave me a hug. I clung to her for a minute because I hated so much to see her go. We've become friends on this long, slow trip, cooking over fires together and taking turns watching the children.

We waved good-bye as their carts disappeared over a high hill. Vincent will be back tomorrow and stay until the goods are on the steamboat. Then he can give us directions.

Tuesday, November 10, 1846

"You need to find shelter right away," Mrs. Jackson warned me today. "We could have a snowstorm any day."

The boys and I walked up and down the cold streets looking for a place. Most buildings seemed to be occupied, even those in very poor condition. I found a place down the street from the well that looked empty. I knocked, but there was no answer. I opened the door very slowly, and no one was inside. The boys and I stepped inside quietly.

"Pee-ugh," Pierre said. "We wouldn't want to stay here. It smells. Squirrels and rabbits have been living here. Birds can fly right in." He pointed to a hole in the ceiling.

"We have to find some place," I said. Papa has just been sitting around the fire with the teamsters ever since we arrived.

I went to talk to Mr. Jackson. He pointed to that same rough-looking little shack. "There's no one in that cabin this winter. The people who lived there built a new place this fall," he said.

"How can I find out if we can stay there?" I asked.

"We know the people who moved out. It didn't really belong to them, either."

My heart sank. Was that the only place available? I could see why it was abandoned. Light showed through between the logs, and part of the roof was gone.

I was getting very annoyed and short-tempered with Papa. Back at the cart I said, "Papa, where are we going to stay this winter?"

"I haven't had a chance to look, but we'll find some-place," he said cheerfully, looking up from the fire. Papa doesn't seem to worry about anything.

"I met Mr. Jackson from the store, and he says there are not any houses available," I told Papa. "I found an old cabin close to the well where nobody is living. I want you to see it, in case we can't find anything better."

I hated to think we would end up there, but I showed it to Papa anyway. Next we went over to Jackson's Store. Mrs. Jackson confirmed that this was the only empty cabin.

"I know it would be risky for a family to go back north in freezing weather," Mrs. Jackson told Papa, agreeing with him.

We walked back to the cabin and looked at it again. Pierre said he thought it would be nice enough for us over the winter if Papa fixed the roof. He and Armond are anxious to get settled in something other than the cart, I think.

"It would be shelter for a few months," Papa said as he looked around the broken-down cabin. I thought it was a sorry place, compared to our snug little home on the Assiniboine. I felt cold all over, the same way I had felt when Papa told me he had taken the job as a team-ster. I was still angry with Papa. Mama always was patient and kind to him, even when he was thoughtless. I decided Papa must have intended to stay in St. Paul when we left the buffalo hunt. This time I couldn't keep quiet.

"When you took the job as teamster, you knew that winter was coming," I said in a snappish way. Armond's eyes stared wide open at my outburst.

Pierre looked from me to Papa. "Papa, aren't we going to go back home?" he asked.

"I didn't know it would take us so long to get here when I took the job," Papa said. "Now, whether we like it or not, we'll have to wait till spring. I'll cut some bark to put over the holes in the roof."

"Papa, Nokomis said birch bark has to be taken off the trees in the spring or it won't peel off in big pieces," I said.

I guess Papa knew that, too, because he answered, "Then I guess I'll have to find another way to do it." Papa sounded as cheerful as ever.

"It's a good thing you were thinking about a place for us, Josette," he said, finally giving me some credit!

Wednesday, November 11, 1846

The boys and I moved everything we brought from our own cart to the cabin. Pierre and I brought in the trunk. It will be our cupboard and our table until Papa builds some shelves. Papa fixed the roof. He says that with three children to help, he'll chink the logs with moss and leaves in no time.

"We might as well get used to the idea of staying here awhile," Papa said as though he liked that idea.

"We still have a real home in St. Eustache," I said to him. I don't intend to get used to staying here. I think of our cottage by the Assiniboine River with such fondness. It has real glass windows that look out at the river. I always imagine it with Mama making meals for us in front of the fire.

Now I'm trying to do the best with what we've got. Inside our temporary cabin there's a place for each person's bedroll and our new buffalo robes. I laid the biggest one, the one that Sophie's mother gave me, on the floor in front of the fireplace. One can still feel the breezes inside whenever the wind blows. In spite of that, it is much better than sleeping under the cart.

Friday, November 13, 1846

Papa is sawing and patching to get the cabin in shape. It is a good feeling to have a roof over our heads, even though we don't have beds. There is a little space behind the cabin for our ox to stay.

When the cart train is unloaded and Papa has been paid, he says he will put all his time into fixing up this cabin. Papa does not seem angry about the things I said to him.

"You're taking care of us like your Mama would have," he said to me yesterday. I took it as a compliment.

Papa has met some other French Canadians who also came down from the Red River and live here now. We're going to have supper with the Desmarias family, who came down here three years ago. They have several children. Two of the girls, Emilie and Lillie, took me to see a spring in the bluff where they wash their clothes. Last night I had the boys and Papa throw their clothes in a heap to be washed today.

When the sun came out this afternoon, the boys helped me carry the clothes and a bucket of hot water to the spring. Mrs. Desmarias gave me a bar of soap she had made from lye and pork fat.

After I scrubbed the clothes in hot water, Emilie and Lillie rinsed them in the spring. They helped wash Papa's and the boys' dirty clothes as well as my old dresses. We draped them over bushes to dry. While the sun was out, the clothes were drying well. But as the afternoon air got cooler and the sun went behind clouds, the clothes started to freeze in strange shapes, as though they were for people with broken arms and misshapen bodies. Emilie, Lillie, and I held them up to our bodies and danced around laughing. The clothes smelled fresh and clean after they finished drying inside.

I suspect that Mrs. Desmarias suggested the girls show me where to wash. We trail riders must really stink! I guess on the trail we stopped noticing body odors. St. Paul does not seem like a place where people notice such things, either, but I want the boys and me to always be as clean as if Papa's sisters in St. Boniface had invited us for dinner.

Saturday, November 14, 1846

The long-awaited steamboat arrived today. Jacques called out orders to unload the carts quickly. Denis got paid enough from Jacques to stay at Jackson's Store the last few nights here, instead of sleeping under the wagon. Most of the other teamsters have already spent their money at the saloons and taverns. There are five or six of those taverns here!

People gathered at Jackson's Store today to wait for the mail to be unloaded. Mr. Jackson made compartments he called pigeonholes in a packing box, and now it's the official post office. This will be the last mail until spring. Many people are sending mail to their friends and relatives in the east.

Last night we had a real feast at the Desmariases' house. When Mr. Desmarias opened the door, warm smells of bread baking greeted us. We met the whole family before we ate. I sat at the table with Emilie and Lillie, and ate vension, cranberries, potatoes, and squash. I felt like we were part of their big family and was homesick for dinners with Papa's relatives in St. Boniface.

After we ate, other families from the Red River came over. I don't remember all their names, but Lavier, Delonias, Gerou, Bibeau, and Bazille were among them. Almost all were Métis, like us. They speak French to each other, but they've lived here long enough that most know English, too. They wanted to know all about us. The teamsters were invited, too, for a sociable evening before they return to Pembina. Jacques, Denis, Charlie, and Stan came, as well as Henriot and Jake.

Papa asked if he could find work making harnesses or doing carpentry. The men told him some of the settlers who come up on the steamboats are lawyers and have money to pay for help. I was beginning to suspect that perhaps Papa does not plan to go home.

"Most times when we French Canadians get together, somebody brings out a fiddle. We push away the table and do a little dancing," Mrs. Desmarias said.

Denis helped push away the table and then stood next me. The fiddlers started to play, and some of the teamsters started tapping their toes in anticipation.

Denis and I kept on talking.

"Have you got all your things unpacked at the cabin?" he asked. "Now that you've found a place, can you help me with lessons until we go back?"

I told him he must come over to see the cabin, even if it is just a makeshift place for the winter. I told him I would like to teach him anytime he came over.

"Do you still want to go back?" he asked. I assured him that I did.

"I wish I could stay here," he said.

I told Denis it was too bad I wasn't a boy, so I could

go back with the teamsters. I only halfway meant it, though. I like being a girl when he smiles. It makes me feel warm all over. I don't know if he thinks of me as a girl or a woman, but I am sure he likes me. As we spoke, I felt as though we were the only people in the room.

When the dancing started, it was the dances we knew from home. Denis and I got into the lines, and each time we met, he smiled at me again. I noticed, though, that he smiled at all the girls. I'm sure Emilie and Lillie also like him.

There were some other young men in the lineup who seemed nice and acted very interested in talking to me. A couple were teamsters from Red River, and the others were from here, I think. We danced to the tunes all evening and had a merry time.

Tuesday, November 17, 1846

Emilie and Lillie took me for a walk today. Behind the narrow streets and shops by the boat landing are high stone banks. I touched the banks and found they are not stone, but sand that brushes off with a touch. It's called sandstone. The Mississippi River is much wider than at the forks where the Assiniboine joins the Red River. I'll have to watch Armond because the current is strong and would pull him right under. It's not a good place for Pierre to fish. Papa told him he must be very careful if he tries it. Everything seemed safer up north, and we lived a more settled life there.

Wednesday, November 18, 1846

Denis stopped by to see our cabin, and I spent the evening teaching him how to read a few words in French, because that's what I know best. I showed him how to write his name, and he wrote it at least twenty times. I invited him for supper tomorrow. It will be our last chance to see him before he goes back to the Red River Settlement. I want it to be a meal he will remember until next summer, so I'm going to make an apple pie. I told Denis that Lillie and Emilie are going to show me the Indian mounds that are on top of the sandstone cliffs Sunday afternoon.

Sunday, November 22, 1846

Denis came over early and asked if Lillie, Emilie, and I would like a ride to the Indian mounds in the cart and horse he's going to take back up the trail. We're keeping our own cart and ox with us so we have a way to get around. The boys stayed with Papa because he wanted them to help him.

I was going to sit in front with Denis for the ride, but Emilie jumped up ahead of me. I sat behind Denis with Lillie and tried to be cheerful. Denis was very gallant and acted as though he liked us all. No favoritism. I had so wanted to get special notice. We chattered the whole way. I don't remember what we talked about, because even though I was a little irked by Emilie, I was excited.

At the top of the cliff, there were about a hundred Indian mounds. Lillie said that the Dakota and Ojibwe who live here say the mounds cover the graves of ancient chiefs.

"This is the most beautiful sight I have ever seen," I exclaimed when we got out of the cart. "It's the highest place I have ever been." From the mounds we could see far across the river to where smoke rose from the Dakota village. In the other direction we could just barely see the village of St. Anthony. The chiefs have a fine place to rest forever. That's what Emilie said.

I looked up and down the river, with the trees growing down to the water and the little settlement of St. Paul below. From a high vantage point the little ramshackle buildings don't look so bad. Even though I am still angry with Papa, I can almost believe this might be a pleasant place to live.

"In the summer we picnic here sometimes," Lillie said.

"Mama doesn't like it, because all these mounds are graves of dead people," Emilie said. The wind was cold, and we started to shiver even though the sun was out. I was glad we had a ride back down. This time Lillie jumped up beside Denis and made a face at her sister.

By the time we got back to the cabin, Papa and Pierre had caught fish for supper. To go with the fish, I baked squash and made corn bread. The apple pie didn't turn out as good as the one we had at the trading post on the trail, but Denis said it was delicious. I asked him if I could send letters back with him to my teachers, and he said that he'd be glad to deliver them. I went right over to Jackson's Store to buy paper. It's nice to live in a village where we can go to the store when we need to.

Papa and Denis talked about the people and jobs here while Pierre and Armond teased and pestered them. Denis said he wants to come back with the big cart train in the spring. He's sure he'd be hired now that he's had experience. Denis lives with his uncle near St. Boniface and helps him; but the uncle can't afford to pay him, so he'll never be able to afford a place of his own if he stays there.

November 22, 1846
Dear Mlles Nolin,

I hope that you received the letter I sent you from the buffalo hunt, so that you knew I did not expect to get back to school when it started. Now I am writing to you from St. Paul on the Mississippi River. This is the northernmost point that riverboat traffic can come to because of a large waterfall a few miles farther north. It was named the St. Anthony Falls by Father Hennepin. Papa was engaged by Norman Kittson as a teamster, along with several others, to bring furs from Pembina down to be loaded on steamboats. Papa feels it would be dangerous to bring me and my brothers back during the winter. I very much hope we will be able to return next summer.

Please greet all my friends at school. How is work on the dictionary proceeding?
Your friend and grateful pupil,
Josette Dupre

I was sad when it was time for Denis to say good-bye. He shook hands with Papa and gave the boys a hug. I handed him letters to the Nolin sisters, to White Cloud, and to Great-Aunt Cecile, telling her to expect Sophie to ask for cooking lessons. I thanked him for taking the letters and wished him well on the return trip. I also said I looked forward to seeing him when the cart train returns, if we are still here.

"See you in the spring," he said as our hands touched. He had a sweet, warm smile on his face. I hope he will miss me as much as I will miss him. I thought he wanted to kiss my lips, but he didn't with Papa and the boys standing there. He bent down and kissed my hand instead.

How will I ever be able to wait till he comes back?

Monday, November 23, 1846

We all went down to the landing this foggy morning to wave good-bye to Denis and the rest of the teamsters. I pray that there will be no bad blizzards for them.

Jacques came over and said he appreciated the help I had given him on the trail. I told him I was glad to have been part of the team and will look for him next spring. I think he needs to find a wife, and hope he finds one in St. Boniface.

The streets were empty as we made our way back to the cabin. I'll miss Denis and even some of the friendly teasing of the teamsters. Branches were bare and black. The town that felt so lively and friendly yesterday now seemed empty and forlorn.

By the time I got back to the cabin, I felt melancholy. I mulled over and over all that had happened to us since we left St. Eustache.

Pierre has grown taller and stronger over the months since we started down the trail. He seems more grown-up. He's only eight, but he saw Augustin get crushed under the wheels of a cart and stood up with us to a buffalo herd and made it change course.

I can't decide about Papa. By coming here he's settled down, he says. He had been used to traveling on the rivers as a voyageur, then he learned that being a cart driver was not as hard on his arms and legs. He didn't have to paddle a canoe or run over the portages with all that weight on his back. He could even ride on the cart some of the time, but I know he's glad that the long trail ride is over.

I can't see what's ahead for me. I just wish I could

finish school. There are many things I could do if I had more schooling.

Armond is still a little boy. He follows me, Pierre, or Papa wherever we go. I know that Armond needs a mother. When I think about this, I can feel his soft arms around my neck. I know I'm not ready to leave them alone when I remember Mama's last words: "Take good care of them, Josette."

Thursday, November 26, 1846

Papa has been out getting wood so that we will have a supply for the next few months. Papa cuts down whole trees, and he and Pierre saw them into pieces.

"Come, Pierre, let's go out and cut more wood," he said again this morning. We have a big stack behind the cabin now, but Papa wants still more.

"I saw the size of the woodpiles that the Jacksons and Desmariases have, so I know we need more wood," Pierre said, trying to sound grown-up. He's quit wearing his sling, and his arm seems to be all right. I told him he should not carry wood with it. He admitted it hurts if he tries.

The fireplace takes more wood than the stove we left in Canada. With all the air holes in this house, we need to keep the fire blazing most of the time. I realize it's a poor old shanty, but Papa says he'll keep improving it. We'll soon be used to it, even if we won't ever be proud of it.

We don't have a barn here, so Papa put some poles in the ground a few feet from the cabin to make a lean-to for the ox. Papa and Pierre cut hay, tied it into bales, and piled it between the poles to make a wall. Then they laid some pieces of bark on top for a roof so the ox can stay warm.

8. A Whole Winter with No School

Monday, November 30, 1846

I like going to the well every day for water because that's where I meet our neighbors. Today I learned some devastating news.

"Where is the school building?" I asked Mrs. Jackson this morning.

"There is no school in St. Paul," she said, "but we hope to have one soon." I already knew there was a shortage of buildings, but no school?

Mrs. Jackson says there was a lady who had taught school for a while last year, but she got married. Then Mr. Cowden, who worked for Mr. Jackson, thought about starting a school; but he hasn't done it yet. If the parents can read, Mrs. Jackson said, they teach their children a little in the evenings.

"Most children run around the streets during the day, getting into mischief," she said. "A few parents are very concerned. I know Mrs. Irvine is, and she has been trying to get others interested in getting a teacher."

I could hardly believe what she was saying. If we had stayed in St. Eustache, I would still be going to school every day, and so would Pierre. Whatever is going to happen to Armond if he doesn't get to go to school?

I woke up during the night and couldn't go back to sleep. Papa may be happy now, but what kind of a chance are we going to have in this world? I can't make him understand how important school is. Papa thinks that even though he has almost no schooling, he's doing all right.

Tuesday, December 1, 1846

At the Jackson store one of their upstairs roomers has left some books for safekeeping. They are biographies of Napoleon, George Washington, and Ben Franklin, and a copy of *Lives of the Presidents*. Mrs. Jackson has let me borrow any I want to read.

I've been thinking about the long winter months

and the fact that there is no school. I've decided to teach Armond letters and numbers this winter. I'm glad I brought a slate with me. It will be something to keep him busy. I don't think he should just be playing on the street. Most of the time it is going to be too cold to go outside, anyway. I'd like to get Pierre to do some schoolwork, too, but I don't think he'd like me for a teacher. He already thinks I boss him too much.

Thursday, December 3, 1846

Papa has been up on the roof covering all the gaps. We stand inside and tell him where light shines through. Sure enough, Papa couldn't get birch bark to come off in big pieces this time of year. He found some bark that's brittle and hopes that a layer of of pine pitch will keep it from leaking.

Meantime, I cook, keep the fire burning, and take care of Armond. I try to be cheerful, but can't always be. If Papa only would have listened to me.

Tuesday, December 15, 1846

We haven't been to Mass since we left St. Eustache. At the store I heard that Father Ravoux will come this month to say Mass in the chapel named St. Paul's. Before the chapel was built, St. Paul was called Pig's Eye after Pierre Parrant, who has only one eye. He sold whiskey to the Indians and to the soldiers at the fort, even though he was ordered to stop. When Parrant and a few others wouldn't stop selling whiskey, the commandant ordered all the people out of the homes they had built near Fort Snelling. They had to move downriver, to the place that is now called St. Paul. Pig's Eye Parrant was ordered out of the area, but he still loads his boat with whiskey, paddles up to the fort, and sells to the soldiers and Indians. Papa says he was a troublemaker as a voyageur but that they'll probably never catch him.

Even though the settlers were forced to move downriver to St. Paul, everyone is invited back to Fort Snelling at Christmastime for a big feast.

Saturday, December 26, 1846

We rode with the Desmarias family out to Fort Snelling for the big party. We piled onto one cart with a buffalo blanket over us. Sleigh bells were ringing as we rode over the frozen river. There was a true feast at the fort. Ham, turkey, buffalo tongue, and venison were set out on long tables. Cranberries and nuts from the forest were served. After the dinner musicians brought out their fiddles, and we danced late into the night. I pulled my hair back on the sides and fastened it with a clip like Mlle Marguerite fixed hers. It makes me feel grown-up and pretty. There were not many women there. I had many soldiers to dance with. Lillie and Emilie did, too. They introduced me to the Irvine family. I can't help but wonder what Denis is doing tonight, and if girls were waiting to dance with him, just like the soldiers were with me.

Friday, January 1, 1847

New Year's Day is called Kissing Day here. We used to call it that at home, too. It's a French custom. Lillie and Emilie came over, and we walked through the town and stopped at each shop. Merchants had little gifts for us. We stopped by, bowed, and said, *"Bonjour"* and *"Bonne année."* We offered our hands or cheek for a kiss. Then we were given cake and a drink of colored sweet water. One place gave us pieces of soap. The boys went, too, and were given candy.

Friday, January 15, 1847

It's every bit as cold here as it was at home, even though we're much farther south. Everyone says, "You must be used to this!" They don't realize how cold we get in our leaky cabin. When it snowed last night, we got a thin layer of snow on our blankets. Papa said that was just because it was so windy last night, and that it might not happen again. I've given up being angry with Papa. It does no good.

Since the river is frozen, steamboats are not able to come up from Prairie du Chien. People miss the sound of the steamboat bell.

Monday, January 18, 1847

It warmed up this afternoon, so we walked out to see Rosalie at Vincent's brother's place. She welcomed each of us with a hug, even Pierre. So did the children. Veronica wouldn't leave my side the whole time. Rosalie says they'll be staying with Vincent's brother until spring.

"When I saw this cabin, I couldn't believe that someone would live in a place so filthy," Rosalie said. "I wonder if that man will ever find a wife," she said with a grin.

The cabin is not much better than the one we moved into, although she has scrubbed the inside. Her baby is due soon.

Friday, January 22, 1847

Every day Pierre stacks more wood into the fireplace. He is so bored he is even willing to work on his lessons; but he's impatient with me when I try to help him. He asks Papa first. Even though Papa doesn't read very well, he is pretty good at numbers. Papa has him measure wood, as if he were building something. Pierre sees that it is important to know that. Armond is learning his letters quickly, and is proud to write his name. I think I'd like teaching better if my students didn't know me so well.

Monday, February 1, 1847

Pierre has given us such a scare that I can barely sit down to write. He went outside in a snowstorm without telling us where he was headed. I didn't know where he'd gone or when he would come back. We were all alarmed. Both Papa and I went out to look for him in the middle of the storm. Papa looked farther away from the cabin. I went to the nearest places, the ones we could see. We had to leave Armond by himself. I told him not to put any logs on the fire, just sit and work on his letters while I was gone. I let him use the slate. I wasn't gone long. When I came back, though, Armond was trying to open the door.

"I was just going to look for you and Papa," he said in his little voice. I was fortunate that I got home before he got the door open.

I was relieved when Papa finally came back, even though he hadn't found Pierre.

"Don't put your own life in jeopardy," Marcel Desmarias warned Papa. "It would be terrible to lose your son, but losing you would be worse for your family." When Papa took off his boots, his feet were white and frozen. I put a tub of snow on the floor, and we rubbed his feet with the fresh snow so they wouldn't hurt from thawing out too fast.

Papa said no one he talked to had seen Pierre, but everybody he talked to said they would be on the lookout for him. People around here don't dare stay out in weather like this. Some people said that any eight-year-old would be sensible enough to go to a nearby house and ask for shelter. The wind is brutal tonight.

The wind blew out some of the chinking between the logs that we had stuffed in so carefully a few weeks before. The snow blew right into the cabin again. I kept sweeping it over by the door (I didn't dare open it) so that our nice buffalo rug would stay dry. We worried about Pierre all evening. Finally we lay down on our beds. I tried to sleep but woke up every few minutes, thinking every blast of wind was a knock at the door.

Tuesday, February 2, 1847

Papa and I were both up early. Armond woke up crying. There was still no sign of Pierre. We've all heard of people freezing to death, both here and in the Red River Settlement. Papa went out to look for Pierre again. The snow kept coming down all morning.

In the afternoon the snow finally subsided. We were amazed to see Pierre come stumbling into the cabin.

"Where have you been, Pierre?" Papa demanded. Pierre tried to act as if nothing special had happened. "You've been gone all night in this storm!"

"Papa, it was like this. I walked out to Alexander's place; and before I noticed, the storm was too bad to came back. Rosalie and Vincent said I had to stay. It was too risky to go out. Rosalie started to have pains because her baby was coming." The words tumbled out in a rush.

"Rosalie didn't want Vincent to leave her, so he couldn't try to take me back, either. He was the only person there who could help her. Vincent had helped her when Alexander was born, she said."

I didn't know what to say next. I wanted to scold Pierre, but I hugged him instead. I wanted to go to Rosalie, but she wouldn't want me there right then. Papa said the only sensible thing to do was stay home.

After the snow stopped, it got even colder. Horses breathed huge billows of steam as they passed by. The street was so cold our boots creaked with every step. Pierre didn't dare go outside again.

Saturday, February 6, 1847

When the big storm was over and the roads had been cleared, I went to see Rosalie and the new baby. Having babies isn't hard for her, she said, and Vincent makes a good midwife.

She looked over at Veronica and said, "The first one was the scary one." The baby was sleeping, but Veronica picked her up and handed her to me. She was so tiny and red. I remembered the last time I held a baby. It was when we brought my baby sister back from Nokomis's village in the canoe. I kept my head down, looking at Rosalie's baby's tiny face. Tears filled my eyes. I thought about how unfair it was that Mama did not survivie when Amilie was born.

"I felt like calling this baby Travelina, after all the traveling she's done," Rosalie joked. "But we didn't. We named her Marie." Veronica says it is fun to take care of a new baby.

Then I told Rosalie the news I had learned. "Mrs. Jackson told me that there is no school in St. Paul."

"I can't believe it," she said. Her children had gone to school in Canada, just like Pierre and I had.

After visiting Rosalie and seeing how restless her children were, I suggested that her children come to our cabin for lessons. I knew it wouldn't be a real school, and I wouldn't be a real teacher, but it would be better than nothing.

Monday, February 15, 1847

Veronica, Julie, and Alexander came to our cabin for lessons today. The boys study better with other children. I wish we had schoolbooks. At least we have paper and pencils donated by Mrs. Jackson.

Veronica wants to catch up on the school she missed. I don't have lesson plans like a real teacher would. Today I asked her to write an essay describing her home in St. Boniface. After thinking a minute, she bent her curly head down and went to work, using the wood box for a desk.

Julie is trying to learn, but everything distracts her. She rushes to look out the door every time a sleigh goes by, and offers to help me every time I stand up.

I'm worried that Alexander will catch Pierre's notions about not liking school. Rosalie won't thank me for that! At least Rosalie can have a little time alone with the new baby. The children will come two days a week at first, and we'll see how it goes from there.

Tuesday, February 23, 1847

I know how to make bread now because Lillie and Emilie and I had a lesson from their mother this week. Mrs. Desmarias keeps out a little dough for a yeast starter each time she bakes. The yeast just keeps multiplying between batches. She showed us how to knead the dough and then put it aside in a warm place.

Mrs. Desmarias says that all girls need to learn how to

make bread, and there's no better time than a winter day. It made me think about Great-Aunt Cecile's offer to teach me bread making. I wondered if Sophie ever went over to see her and if Antoine's arm has healed. I thought of all my friends to the north. Do they ever think of me, so far away?

We talked and sang while we waited for the dough to rise. Emilie said she wishes they could have a piano; but as of now, nobody in St. Paul has one. They know most of the songs I know because all French Canadians sing them. Emilie wanted to sing "Send Her Along" *(Envoyons de l'avant, nos gens!)* in French because it tells of girls singing about their beaux. Lillie likes a young man who came here from the East last summer, but she has beaux among the French Canadians, too. She's always thinking about boys.

Friday, February 26, 1847

Papa gets work whenever he can. He gets cross when he is at home too many days in a row. Last night he made a harness, using the buffalo sinew, cords, and hides we had saved.

I bring snow inside to melt for washing dishes and clothes. It takes a long time for clothes to dry inside our drafty cabin. The weather was cold today, and the river is still frozen; but spring is on its way, Mrs. Jackson says.

Monday, March 1, 1847

Today I met Mr. Irvine's family. Mrs. Jackson sent me up to their house with groceries because she thinks I should get to know the Irvine girls. The Irvines have the nicest house in this town. It's made of board siding like some of the houses in St. Boniface. It's on the edge of a large stand of tamarack trees that Mr. Irvine cuts and sells for lumber.

After I knocked on the door and explained that Mrs. Jackson had sent me with groceries, Mrs. Irvine invited me in to meet her daughters. Her oldest, Amanda, is thirteen, too. I hope I can get better acquainted with her. She knows Lillie and Emilie already. All of Mrs. Irvine's children are girls. Mary is eleven; Cythera, seven; Cleopatra, five; and the baby, Viola, is three.

She asked me if I'd been to school, and I told her about the one at St. Eustache and about my teachers, Angelique and Marguerite Nolin.

"You have been very fortunate," she said. "My daughters have not been to school since we moved here two years ago. Only the two oldest went to school in Prairie du Chien when we lived there. I told the doctor who lives across the river that if he could get a teacher to come to St. Paul, she could stay with us," she said.

I was getting excited and said without thinking, "If a teacher doesn't come soon, I could teach the younger girls along with Armond, Pierre, and Rosalie's children." I think she liked the idea, but I forgot to tell her that our classes are in French.

I was afraid that the Irvines wouldn't like me because I'm of mixed blood. Here many people call us half-breeds, instead of Métis. Still, most are very friendly.

Monday, March 15, 1847

Amanda, Mary, Cythera, and Cleopatra Irvine came here for classes this morning. They were all dressed up with ribbons in their hair. They wore pinafores, except for Amanda, who wore a skirt and blouse. I was embarrassed because I'm not a real teacher and this isn't a real school. At least the boys had combed their hair. I have to speak slowly so that everyone understands me. The Irvine girls don't understand French, but afterward I repeat in English. Usually, though, I just talk to each child separately about his or her lesson. I have decided to have Veronica and Mary in a class just for them because they're both eleven. They also help the younger ones read and make letters. It makes them feel more grown-up.

Amanda Irvine is anxious to catch up with all the things she's missed in the last two years. She told me they have some books at home, and she has read most of them. She offered to let me borrow them. After the children went home, I wrote plans for the next day. It is keeping me very busy.

No steamboat has made it up the river yet this spring, so there has been no mail for four months. It doesn't seem as though spring is coming very soon. Snowbanks are still high, and though the snow melts some during the day, it all freezes again at night. Mrs. Jackson has asked me to help her put supplies on the shelves when the first steamer arrives. When the mail arrives, I'll also help her put it in the pigeonholes.

Thursday, April 15, 1847

Today was a bad day at school. Even though there were still piles of snow that had turned to frozen ice, the air seemed warm and it felt like spring.

"We don't have to go to your school anymore," Pierre said in front of the other children. I was very annoyed. The boys ran outside without permission and made little trenches in the snowbanks to drain water down to the river. More ice melts every day. Later, when Papa came home, Veronica and I walked across town to the Irvines' house. Amanda had invited us over to make taffy.

I told Mrs. Irvine about the trouble I had with my students today. She laughed and said, "Even an experienced teacher would have trouble keeping students in school on a beautiful day like today." That was nice of her to say, but I know a real teacher would have been able to keep her students interested.

Thursday, April 22, 1847

A steamboat arrived today! I dismissed school as soon as we heard the whistle. The children began shouting and ran outside, leaving the door wide open. Most everyone in town went down to the landing at the foot of Jackson Street. The mailbag was taken ashore first. It's the only mail people have had since November.

Now I have a job for a few days. People can hardly

wait to see if they have received letters. Lots of boxes came for the store. I won't have classes in the afternoon tomorrow, because I want to help Mrs. Jackson.

The snow is gone except in spots the sun doesn't reach. Grass is turning green. Papa heard that the cart train will start from Pembina as soon as the grass is tall enough for the animals to graze. I hope Denis was hired as one of the teamsters. I can hardly wait to see him. I'm worried that I'm not the only one who can hardly wait. I hope he brings letters from White Cloud and the Nolin sisters.

Monday, May 3, 1847

Papa announced today that he has bought a small piece of land up the hill from the landing at Jackson's Store. I'm so angry, I can hardly speak. He acts jocular and proud of himself. How could he have done this without even mentioning it to his children?

"What about our home in St. Eustache?" I asked Papa. "Aren't we going back there?"

"We'll go back sometime," he said. "But this town is filling up with new peple who need houses and other things I can make. This is an exciting place to be. More settlers will get off the steamboat every time one arrives."

Papa has had many offers of work, more than he can handle. He wants to build a new cabin soon with money he has saved from his odd jobs. When we decide to go back, there will be plenty of people who will want to buy this new cabin, Papa says.

All winter long I worried that this day would come.

Papa insisted that we walk up the hill with him to see the land he bought. It is on high ground, but I could still see the river from there. On the property there is a spring coming out of the side of the hill, so water wouldn't need to be hauled far.

Papa spread out his arms to take in the whole plot of land and asked, "Where shall I build the cabin?"

Pierre shrugged his shoulders. At first, I decided not to say anything, since I hadn't been asked about any of the other planning. Papa doesn't even know that he has hurt my feelings. Finally, I gave up and said that the door should face the river so that we could look all the way down to the water. I stood at the spot where I thought it should be. Now he thinks I'm in agreement with his decision to stay here, but I am not.

"That's good, Josette," he said. "That would be south-facing, and we would get warmth in through the door in nice weather." Pierre said he hoped we would have glass windows. I do, too.

"I'll put glass windows in the front on either side of the door, but in the back we might have stretched hide windows like we have now until we have more money," Papa said.

There were little blue violets growing at the trunk of a tree near where he plans to build. They were so blue and tiny, they would be easy to miss. Papa's going to start building this week so that he can put the roof on in the next few weeks while the birch bark is at its best.

I will be glad to leave our drafty old cabin, of that I am sure. But I still have a grudge against Papa for not taking us back to St. Eustache so I can finish school. Papa just ignores my feelings. If there was someone to take care of Armond and Pierre, I might go back on my own and hope that my dream of going to Montreal would still be possible.

Monday, May 10, 1847

Papa, with a little help from Pierre, cut down trees on our land for the cabin. Armond and I went to watch, mostly because I want to be sure Papa leaves some trees near the cabin for shade.

Monday, May 17, 1847

Today Vincent came over to help Papa and so did Marcel Desmarias. The cabin is going up very fast. Armond and I went to see what we could do. After the men cut the branches off the tree trunks, the boys and I put them in a big pile.

I believe Vincent plans to build a house as soon as they have land.

Tuesday, June 1, 1847

The side walls of the cabin are up. Papa is building the cabin the French-Canadian way. He has set tall posts with grooves in the ground at each corner. Then he drops grooved logs in place between the tall posts. After he smoothes the outside wall, it doesn't look like an ordinary log house anymore. Papa gets better at building houses each time he does it. He is so proud of this new house, I worry he won't want to sell it so we can move back to St. Eustache. I have to admit it is a much better house than the one he built on the Assiniboine River.

I love the little spring that flows out of the ground by the rocks near the new house. It will be so nice to have good, clear water close by. Even though I don't want to admit it, it is a good place for us until we go home.

Rosalie and the children came to see the progress. The baby has grown and looks different each time I see her. Papa is going to help them build their new cabin.

Rosalie has planted a garden with seeds she brought along with her. Then I remembered I had brought the corn and squash seeds Mama had saved. I got Papa and Pierre to dig up the sod for a small garden. It is very hard to break the soil for the first time. It will be fun to watch the plants come up. I'm sure I planted too many for us, but if Rosalie and Vincent get land and their new house this year, they won't have had time to plant another garden this season.

Tuesday, June 15, 1847

We spend every warm day at the new cabin now. Amanda Irvine walked up with me to see it. She loves it, especially the view from the front. Our house won't be as grand as the Irvines', but still, it's much better than most other houses around here.

Friday, July 2, 1847

We're expecting the Red River cart train to come rolling in any day now. I hope Denis will be one of the teamsters. Before I go to sleep, I often remember how strong his arms were when he pulled me from the river. I get a tingle down my spine when I think about the day I handed him the letters to take back. Sometimes I dream that he kissed me on the lips. I know he didn't, but I've thought about it so many times, it seems like he really did.

9. Miss Harriet Bishop and the Cart Train Arrive

Thursday, July 8, 1847

Today the cart train finally arrived. I was at our old cabin when I heard the carts squeaking toward the landing. This cart train is much longer than the one we came down on last fall. The trappers must have had a good season. One hundred and twenty-one carts came this time.

Armond and Pierre were very excited. I was the most excited of all but tried to be calm, just in case Denis didn't come. We recognized many of the drivers from last year. I think everyone who lives in St. Paul came outside to wave. I saw Lillie and Emilie craning their necks to see if they knew any of the drivers. They kept waving frantically at several teamsters they must have known before. I noticed Amanda Irvine looking at the whole procession, too. Papa was on the hill building the new cabin, so Pierre ran to bring him the news.

Then I saw Denis. He seemed taller and even more handsome than he had last fall. He looked my way with his big smile and waved but had to keep on leading his carts. My heart started to pound, and I felt shy. Maybe a handsome man like he is has found a girlfriend in St. Boniface by now. Someone prettier than me. Oh, I hope not.

Friday, July 9, 1847

Veronica and I went down by the landing, walking past cart after cart until we found the ones Denis has been leading.

"Hello. I told you I'd be back," he said with his familiar big smile before I had a chance to say anything. We stood and talked to him for a while, and I felt tingly all over. I pointed to our old cabin and asked him if he could come over when he was free.

"I have to stay with the carts until we can unload, just like last fall. They're afraid of looters. The earliest will be tomorrow, they say."

I had baked bread this morning, so I made Denis a sandwich and brought it to him by the carts.

"You know how good fresh food tastes after weeks on the trail, don't you?" he said. I loved seeing his warm smile again.

Sunday, July 11, 1847

This afternoon Denis was finally able to leave the carts. I packed a picnic lunch, and we took it up the hill so he could see the new house.

The boys ran ahead, excited to have Denis with us again. Every time Denis and I tried to talk, the boys wanted his attention. I showed him the spring and the violets growing under the tree. The boys competed to show him a spiderweb, raccoon tracks, and a bird's nest they had found.

"Well, have you waited long enough?" Denis asked as he reached into his pocket. He brought letters for me from White Cloud and the Nolin sisters. He also brought one from Sophie. I sat down under the tree and read them while Papa showed Denis his building project.

April 14, 1847

Dear Josette,

I hope your long trip down the trail went well. I was glad to get your letter delivered by Denis.

Antoine is not well at all. The shoulder where he was shot is painful and stiff. The hand that was dragged on the ground and stomped on by horses is almost useless. He has become dejected because he thinks he will not be able to earn a good living.

I do my best to encourage him, but he insists that we put off our wedding. How can he insist on not getting married when we love each other so much? I feel worse because my father agrees with Antoine.

I took the note you gave me to your great-aunt and told her I would like to come over and learn more about baking when Antoine is better.

With love from your buffalo-hunt friend,
Sophie

The Nolin sisters each wrote a note. They had received both the letter I sent from the buffalo hunt and the one Denis brought them. They reminded me to keep studying and reading, even if I'm not in school anymore. White Cloud says she is now their helper at school and very happy about that, even though she misses me. I put the letters into my pocket to reread. After I finished reading, we spread a blanket under the tree that had the violets and laid out the food I had brought. We could see the river and the stores below us.

"This is a fine spot you've found here," Denis told Papa. "I'll come up and help you tomorrow." Denis said it will be three weeks before the cart train goes back to Pembina, and Denis will come to help Papa every day.

Monday, July 12, 1847

Today while I was bringing lunch to Papa and Denis at the new cabin, I saw a lady dressed as Mlle Marguerite used to, with a shiny black skirt and black blouse with a white collar. Nobody in St. Paul dresses like that! She is younger than Mrs. Irvine or Mrs. Jackson, and wears her black hair pulled back into short ringlets. She looked puzzled as she stood above the landing viewing the carts and all the unkempt and dirty teamsters lying on the ground.

"Mademoiselle, can I help you?" I asked.

"Thank you. I've just arrived in St. Paul and don't know my way yet," she said in a formal way.

Then she looked at me and changed to a friendly tone. "Do you know where all those carts come from?"

That was the easiest question she could have asked me. I told her they came down on the Red River Trail with furs to be loaded on steamboats. She seemed relieved that I could answer her, even if my English was not perfect.

Then she asked, "Do you know Mr. John Irvine?"

I said I did.

"Could you please tell me where to find him?" she asked.

I pointed in the direction of the Irvines' house and said I would show her the way. As we walked, she asked questions.

"Do you know how many children live in St. Paul?" she said.

I named all I could think of—the Irvine girls, Lillie and Emilie and their brothers, Rosalie's children, and five or six others I've met.

"How long have you lived here?" she asked. I told her we came from Canada last fall and usually spoke French.

Before we got to the Irvine house, I saw Mr. Irvine supervising a crew cutting down trees. When I pointed him out, she walked over to him and said in a clear, distinct voice: "Mr. Irvine, my name is Harriet Bishop. I've come to St. Paul to start a school."

Mr. Irvine removed his hat and said, "You're very welcome here, ma'am."

"I decided to come after reading the letter Dr. Williamson sent East, explaining the needs in St. Paul. I've just arrived. Dr. Williamson suggested I contact you to find out how to proceed."

Mr. Irvine paused for a moment and seemed a bit flustered. Then he said, "We did not have word that you were coming. My family has great need of a teacher, and my wife will be happy you are here." Miss Bishop smiled at that. "My wife had asked Dr. Williamson to help find someone to conduct a school," he added.

"I stopped first at the Dakota village across the river to meet Dr. Williamson," Miss Bishop said. "He said that you would help find a building where we could begin the school."

Mr. Irvine seemed disconcerted and paused for a moment. "We have been waiting a long time." He asked me to take Miss Bishop to their house. I walked with her along the path through the trees to the Irvines' front door.

When Mrs. Irvine opened the door, I said, "Mrs. Irvine, this is Miss Harriet Bishop."

Before I could say anything else, Miss Bishop reached out her hand and said, "Mrs. Irvine, I know you've been waiting for a teacher. I have just arrived in St. Paul to start a school."

They seemed very pleased to meet each other. Miss Bishop met Amanda and the younger Irvine daughters and asked them questions about their school lessons. The girls were very excited. The littlest one, Viola, hid her face in her mother's skirt.

"I assured Dr. Williamson that if he got a schoolteacher to come, she would be able to live at our house," Mrs. Irvine said. She said they would move one of the beds so the girls would all sleep in one room and the teacher could have a room of her own.

Miss Bishop said she thought it best to go back to the Dakota village until the school building was found and the room for her was ready. I think she was afraid of the cart train and the unkempt look of some of the drivers.

After Mrs. Irvine served tea, Miss Bishop and I

walked back down to the landing. I hoped Miss Bishop didn't understand French, because the words the teamsters jokingly called out when we passed by would have embarrassed her.

Wednesday, July 14, 1847

I have so much to write about now, I barely have time to put it all down. Armond and I met Mr. Irvine as we walked along the bluff this morning. He was asking about buildings that could be used for a school. Buildings are even more scarce than before now that more people have arrived. Many people are still camped outside with their belongings.

Mr. Irvine said, "I haven't been able to find a building that isn't being used." I don't know what he will do. A new family is already waiting to move into our old cabin.

"My wife expects me to find something suitable. If I don't, she's afraid the new teacher won't stay," he continued.

After looking most of the day, Mr. Irvine decided to use an old building on the river bluff between Jackson's Store and the Irvines' house. Long ago it was Scott

Campbell's cabin, they say, but it was last used as a blacksmith's shop. I don't think it's nice enough to be a school. Angelique and Marguerite Nolin would never have agreed to open a school in a building like that.

Monday, July 19, 1847

Miss Bishop came back across the river yesterday with her trunk and moved into the Irvines' house. Pierre heard that she's ready to start the school this week. I told him he must go.

"I'm going to stay here at home with Armond," he said. "He's not ready to go yet." However his curiosity eventually got the best of him, and he went to see what was happening. He said that Miss Bishop spoke to the class in English and it was hard for him to understand, even though he's learned a lot of English since we came here. Except for the Irvine girls, most of the children can't understand the teacher. Most speak French. There were also several Ojibwe children and some Sioux. Pierre said he listened from the doorway for a while and then raised his hand.

"Yes, what is it?" Miss Bishop asked. "Please come in and sit down because school has begun."

"I know someone who can help the children under-stand what you are saying," Pierre said.

"How is that?" she asked.

"Most children here speak no English," Pierre told her. "Wait, I will bring help."

Pierre ran back to the cabin to get me. I took Armond along, and we went up to the little building. The inside was in worse condition than our old cabin. While the class was waiting for me, Miss Bishop had sent some of the children to get pine boughs from the trees nearby. They hung them on the walls to bring the fresh pine smell inside.

As soon as we arrived at the door, Miss Bishop rec-ognized me. She even remembered my name.

"It's nice to meet you again, Josette," Miss Bishop said. "This boy tells me you may be able to help me. It seems that some of these children do not understand English."

When I told her that I was still learning English, she asked me why.

"I have spoken French all my life. My mother was Ojibwe," I said. Then I explained to her that I had trans-lated Ojibwe words for the teachers at St. Eustache.

"Class, I now believe that you will all be able to un-derstand me," she said. When she said, "Good morning, scholars," in English, I repeated it in French and then in

Ojibwe, just as I had in class at St. Eustache. After that I repeated everything she said.

There were Dakota children who couldn't understand anything. I had only learned a few words of Dakota from Adele. If the Dakota children come back to school, I will try to learn more.

"Would you be able to help me at school every day?" Miss Bishop asked. I said I would if Armond could come to school.

I placed my hand on his shoulder and said, "He can print his name already."

"Of course, Armond, we want you to come to school." Miss Bishop smiled at us, and I knew I was going to like St. Paul a lot better now.

Friday, July 23, 1847

Miss Bishop had me interpret all week. When she found out about the schooling I had had in St. Eustache, she asked me to help the little ones as well. Though he won't be five until fall, Armond fits in better than children who have never been to school. Learning his letters and how to count gave him a head start. Interpreting is hard for me, but I am learning new words. I use the dictionary whenever I can. Miss Bishop brought textbooks with her from Vermont, and I study them whenever I have a little time.

At the end of the day, Miss Bishop announced that the class was invited to come back on Sunday morning to hear Bible stories, but they needed a parent's permission to come.

Sunday, July 25, 1847

Since Papa, Pierre, and Denis were busy at the cabin this morning, Armond and I went to school on Sunday. Only seven other children came.

"When I was a young girl in Vermont," Miss Bishop said, "I read about a lady who went across the ocean to teach children who had never heard of a Sunday School. Now I am a very long way from my home, and I want to teach the children in St. Paul about the Bible." I interpreted for her as I had during the week. I knew some of the stories from school in St. Eustache. Sunday School lasted only an hour. Then I took sandwiches up to the new cabin again for another picnic.

I am much happier now. I always wanted to be a teacher's helper, and now I am one. There are a few good things that have happened in St. Paul. After Mama died I was afraid that everything would turn bad. But I am learning to expect good things, too.

Wednesday, August 4, 1847

Today is my fourteenth birthday. It's been a whole year since we left home. I miss home because of Mama. I still think of it often, and of the school and my teachers. The new cabin will soon be finished. It has a stone chimney and fireplace. Progress on it has slowed because Papa has had so much work to do for other people.

"There's no hurry," Papa said, "as long as the weather is good. We'll have plenty of time to finish," he said. I reminded him that a family is waiting to move into our old cabin.

Last night after Papa and Denis stopped working, Denis stayed for a while. He sat under the tree with me, looking down toward the river as the sun went down. The sky was filled with beautiful shades of salmon and rose, turquoise and blue.

"I'm not going to go back up the trail to St. Boniface," he said. "I didn't sign on for the return trip this time. I'm staying here instead." I felt like my heart skipped a beat. I was thrilled but tried to remain calm. My head filled with questions. Do I want to stay here? What about going to school in Montreal? What about the house I love so much in St. Eustache? Have I given up my dreams?

Denis sleeps above Jackson's Store and works at odd jobs, just like Papa. In the evening he helps Papa finish the new cabin. Denis has made a ladder to go to the cabin's sleeping loft. Later he will build stairs. Sometime he will make the loft into two rooms so that I can have a light on after the boys are asleep. I think about Denis's plan to stay here and wonder about going back up the trail myself. The cabin should be ready for us to move in next week.

Monday, August 30, 1847

We've moved all our things into the new cabin. It is so well built, I should call it a house.

"I can guarantee that this roof won't leak," Papa said last night.

We are so high up on the hill that the clothes flap in the breeze when I hang them to dry. Denis put in two posts so that I can string up a clothesline. I had asked

Papa several times, but he isn't in a rush to do things when I ask him. Denis did it right away to please me.

Last night Papa talked about the stove he had bought for Mama the year before she died. Many of the women in Red River had one. It stood on legs, and we put in wood through a door in the front. We placed the kettles on the flat top when we were cooking. We didn't have to stoop over to stir the pots, and it also kept the house nice and warm. Smoke went up the chimney. If we get another one, it will go opposite the fireplace.

Wednesday, September 1, 1847

Denis came this afternoon with news.

"Mr. Irvine hired me to cut down trees," he said. "It will be a steady job for the whole winter."

"I'm happy for you," I said. "I think Mr. Irvine would be a good person to work for." Denis is glad to have work, but he may be too busy to come up here as much. At least he won't be tempted to go back on the trail anytime soon. I can't help but be a little sad about that, because I was imagining I would run into him in St. Boniface when I am older.

Tuesday, September 7, 1847

The school is going rather well. I still interpret and help the youngest children. Miss Bishop says she is glad I am there to help because most of the students are far behind where they should be in school. When the weather is pleasant, we meet outside.

We look down on an island below and have started to call it Harriet's Island for Miss Bishop.

Friday, October 1, 1847

St. Paul now has a newspaper called *The Minnesota Pioneer*. The headline today was that Mr. J. W. Bass and his pretty wife have opened the Merchants' Hotel. Mrs. Jackson worries that it will take business away from them; but the Jacksons still have the post office, the store, and beds for rent upstairs, so I don't think she should worry. The paper also announced that Dr. John Dewey has moved to St. Paul. Everyone is happy to have a doctor. He is going to open a drugstore, too.

Minnesota is growing. Mr. Jackson thinks it will be made a territory soon. It might even get to be a state someday.

Denis told me that the Irvines invited him over to eat at their house last night, without the other lumberjacks. I know Amanda Irvine has her eye on him. I hope he doesn't return her affections. I'm sure she did her best to be friendly, and Denis would have liked that. He is getting to know Miss Bishop better because she did a lot of talking at the dinner table.

Monday, November 1, 1847

Now that the weather has gotten colder, Miss Bishop comes to school early to start a fire. Mr. Irvine's woodmen have stacked a supply of wood outside. Denis often brings it. Inside the school it is very crowded with new children. None of us like this little room, but I think the crowded school building is harder on Miss Bishop than anyone else.

Soon the ice on the river will stop the steamboats, just like last year. We've gotten used to hearing the steamboat bell twice a month.

Friday, December 3, 1847

Every week there is a dance at someone's house. All the French-Canadian settlers come. Papa loves to dance, and so do I. The fiddlers here are as good as the ones in Canada and play the same merry tunes. The best part is that Denis takes me to the dances. Armond and Pierre play in the bedroom with the other children until they fall asleep. Amanda, being from the East, never comes, and that's all right. She probably wouldn't fit in with us Métis. Some of the other settlers from the East come once in a while. I invited Miss Bishop, and she did come a time or two; but she stopped.

"Josette," she said, "I know it's what you're used to, but with the all the drinking that goes on, I think those parties are nothing but a whiskey hoedown."

From the day she arrived, she has disapproved of people who drink too much. In St. Paul many drunk men sleep in the streets unless it's absolutely freezing. Quite a few of them are teamsters. When we lived in the old cabin, we once found a man sleeping in the shelter with our ox to stay warm.

10. Miss Bishop Plans to Build a Real School

Christmas, December 25, 1847

We all crossed the frozen river to Fort Snelling for Christmas dinner again this year. Miss Bishop rode in the Irvine's sleigh, with all the Irvine girls shaking their sleigh bells. Denis drove the ox and our cart, with Papa, the boys, and me. Denis says he plans to get his own horse and wagon soon so he can make money giving people rides.

Denis was amazed to see the long, festive tables covered with elaborate platters of turkey, frosted ham, buffalo tongue, oyster soup, sardines, cranberry sauce, pastries, and pecans. It was even grander than last year. The soldiers had prepared theatrics and dancing, too. I had told Denis about last year's celebration, but he did not expect it to be as grand as it was. Denis danced all evening. Before the music stopped I think he had danced with every girl there.

Saturday, January 1, 1848

The New Year has begun. We told Miss Bishop all about Kissing Day. Veronica, Rosalie, and I invited her to go with us. We went to all the shops, even new ones that just opened. We each greeted the proprietor, and gave and received a kiss. We were all given little treats. Miss Bishop thinks it is a pleasant custom, if a little quaint.

Miss Bishop is a very busy lady. She wants to make every minute count, she says. She seems older than she is, but maybe it's just because she knows how to take charge. Everyone looks to Miss Bishop to get things done. She is determined to turn St. Paul into a respectable town.

With eight other women, Miss Bishop has started the St. Paul Circle of Industry to raise money to build a new school. Miss Bishop said she will teach me to sew if I go to the Circle meetings. She has also invited Amanda Irvine to come with her mother. With the funds the Circle has raised so far, they made a payment for the first order of lumber. The school building will be twenty-five by thirty feet, and they have been told it can be built for three hundred dollars. The building will be started as soon as the weather improves.

I went along with the women from the Circle of Industry to Fort Snelling to ask the officers to contribute money toward the school. Denis took us in Mr. Irvine's large wagon. Miss Bishop read a letter from Dr. Thomas Williamson of the Dakota Mission across the river, addressed to the National Board of Popular Education. She had first read this letter at a school in the East for teachers. It had convinced Miss Bishop to go West to teach.

Dr. Williamson had written that the settlement named St. Paul was on a high bluff of the Mississippi and had a small chapel. The Dakotas called it *Im-mi-jaska* (white rock) because of the color of the sandstone on which the settlement stands. The village contains a dozen to twenty families. A teacher should be willing to forgo the neatness and elegance of New England towns. She should be free of prejudice on account of color. A teacher should bring books because there is no bookstore within three hundred miles.

After Miss Bishop finished reading Dr. Williamson's letter, the officers asked some questions. I learned that there had been a school at the fort that had been discontinued. Many of the officers were interested in starting another one. They gave a generous donation of fifty dollars.

Tuesday, January 18, 1848

Life is not easy for Miss Bishop. She has been so friendly to people interested in schooling that many think she can solve all of their problems.

This morning some excited people pulled a sled to the school. On the sled was the body of a man who was frozen stiff. He was already dead, and there was nothing Miss Bishop could do. She said the man was probably drunk when he wandered out into the cold.

Miss Bishop resents people in this town who sell liquor. All the shops in St. Paul sell liquor, and Miss Bishop says she is going to do her best to change that. I know many of the Métis drink more alcohol than they should, even Papa does sometimes.

Tuesday, February 1, 1848

Today at the Circle of Industry meeting, I did mending for men who have come here without wives.

Ladies who attend besides Miss Bishop are Mrs. Nancy Irvine, Mrs. Laura Bass, Miss Harriet Patch, and Mrs. Angelina Jackson. I just learned Mrs. Jackson's first name. I think it is such a pretty one. Most of the women are from New England. When the mending is finished, the women make quilts. They are going to make one for each person in the Circle. After that they will make them to sell to raise money to build the new school.

Miss Bishop is fussy about how the stitches are made. She checks the stitching Amanda and I do.

The Circle meets in homes, so I have been inside the homes of most of the ladies. I find it fascinating to see the objects they brought with them on their long trips here. Most brought pictures and books, but some brought carved butter molds and pretty decorations made of hair. At the Irvines' house one day, I saw several interesting books I'd like to read. Because of my French background, the Irvines loaned me a book of eight stories collected by Charles Perrault that includes "Cinderella" and "Sleeping Beauty." They also have a book with a poem called "Account of a Visit from St. Nicholas." Miss Bishop read it to the class and also to the Sewing Circle at Christmastime.

Sometimes I am offered a ride home, but Denis says I should wait for him to come. He brings Mr. Irvine's cart to take Mrs. Irvine and Amanda home, and they invite me, too. He takes me home last, and I often invite him to stay for supper.

Usually he stays for a while after we finish eating. Living in a boardinghouse gets tiresome, he says. We all like to have him stay, but I just love it.

At the Irvines' house Miss Bishop spends many of her evenings doing embroidery and needlepoint at a sewing table she brought from Vermont. It has a hinged cover with a mirror inside. The light from her candle reflects off the mirror to make a much brighter light to sew by in the evening. Sewing is kept inside the cover, and when the cover is closed, it is a small table.

Miss Bishop and Mrs. Irvine had a wonderful surprise for me. They want to make me a dress with extra fabric Mrs. Irvine brought with her when she moved here. Miss Bishop wants to thank me for all the translating I do for her. I don't have a nice dress. I brought some of Mama's things along, but they are too big for me.

Friday, February 11, 1848

Every Friday Miss Bishop invites students to bring their parents and friends to Sunday School. She says that too many in St. Paul think Sunday should be spent hunting, wrestling, drinking, and gambling, mixed in with a little visiting. She believes the Sabbath day should be spent in prayer and quiet reflection. Although she sees room for improvement, she says she is happy she came to Minnesota. She wanted to come to a place where she was really needed.

All the new people who move here want to meet Miss Bishop. Men appear to squire her home from school and to other events. There are very few women here, and she is about the only unmarried one. I think she enjoys the attention most of the time.

Monday, March 13, 1848

After school today I worked on lessons with Amanda Irvine. We are the oldest pupils at the school. I am learning how the United States was formed from the colonies. Miss Bishop and Mrs. Irvine had me try on the new dress they have almost finished. It fits me so well.

Afterward Amanda's little sisters begged us to play school with them. I think they will soon catch up with the schooling they missed. Little Viola wants to do lessons, even though she's only three. She kept pulling on my sleeve, then running behind the door and peeking out. When I offered her a pencil and paper, she came back to the table and crept up on my lap. I kept hoping that Denis would stop at the Irvines' house on an errand, but he didn't. I so hope that he doesn't grow fond of Amanda. Even though he doesn't know English well, he is very handsome.

Rosalie's children are doing fine at school. Most of the Canadian scholars at Miss Bishop's school have been to school before. They stick together. I suppose it's easier for them to speak French to one another after school than to get acquainted with those who speak only English. I've learned a lot of English since I've been here. At the Sewing Circle everyone speaks English.

Sunday, March 19, 1848

Today the weather was very mild, and Denis took me for a ride in the country. There is still snow, but it is crusty and melting. Denis is learning English quickly, but he says reading it is another matter. We went for a visit to New Canada, a place north of town where many of the people from the Red River have settled. Rosalie and Vincent have bought land near there. Denis thinks it would be a fine place to live. He showed me a little hill that he thinks would be a perfect place to build a house. He didn't say anything about whom the house would be for, but I couldn't help think that he might be thinking it could be for us.

Friday, April 14, 1848

A horrible thing has happened at the Irvines' house. I was over there when little Viola ran over to the neighbor's house to play with a kitten. Viola was jumping about in glee when she lost her balance and fell into a pan of hot coals. The screaming little girl was carried back home. I ran to alert the new doctor.

Saturday, April 15, 1848

I stopped by the Irvines' house this morning. Amanda told me her sister screamed the entire night. This morning she is whimpering, but thankfully, she falls in and out of sleep. The doctor says her burns are very extensive.

This has been a terrible week for the Irvine family, and for all their friends and neighbors. Many people want to help, but no one knows what to do.

Miss Bishop is overwhelmed by sadness. She told me that before she knew anyone else, Viola would creep into her room with hugs and questions. Amanda will stay home to help her mother until Viola is better. I have been helping the younger sisters after school so they will stay busy and away from home.

Sunday, April 23, 1848

Today at Sunday School, Miss Bishop told me she has decided to close school temporarily so she can sit by Viola's bedside and relieve Mrs. Irvine and Amanda.

Monday, April 24, 1848

Viola died during the night. Amanda and her sisters are distraught. They can hardly believe what has happened. The whole town is shocked by this terrible accident. There is no pastor in this town yet, although a priest comes every few months. Miss Bishop wept as she read comforting words of scripture beside the grave. Then she prayed for Viola and her family. This incident has filled us all with sorrow.

Monday, May 1, 1848

Miss Bishop has developed a very bad cold, and she's afraid it might be pneumonia. The school has been closed since Viola died, and now Miss Bishop has decided to keep it closed until next fall when the new building is finished.

Miss Bishop sent a message to Dr. Williamson at Kaposia to tell him about her illness. He arranged for a Dakota woman everyone calls Old Betsy to take Miss Bishop across the river in a canoe padded with pine boughs. The doctor even sent over his umbrella to shade her from the sun. I carried Miss Bishop's bag down to the shore. She was coughing and leaned on my arm because she felt weak. I held the canoe steady as she lay down in it. Miss Bishop said she trusts Dr. Williamson will help her return to health.

Friday, May 12, 1848

I received a message from Miss Bishop today. Her pneumonia is gone now. She feels much better and plans to take a trip to Galena, Illinois, and then maybe on to

St. Louis next week. She thinks a short trip will help her gain back her strength.

And this is the most intriguing news. She would like to have me go with her. She hasn't fully recovered, and I would be both a companion and a nurse to her. I can hardly believe it!

It's been about a year and a half since we came down the trail to St. Paul. I know I would love to travel and see a little bit more of the United States. I think I should take this opportunity.

Sunday, May 14, 1848

When I told Papa about the invitation, he didn't answer at first.

"I thought you'd had enough of traveling," he said. I know he was worried about who would cook and care for the boys if I was gone.

"It's a chance to see Galena and maybe even St. Louis," I said. "Will I ever have another chance?"

Papa finally gave me the money for passage. I know that he and the boys can manage all right and that Denis will be there, too. I went to tell Rosalie, and she said she will have Papa and the boys over to eat sometime. I'll make fresh bread before I go and cook a couple of meals for the first days I'm gone. Papa can do some cooking. I'm sure he did when he traveled the rivers. I'm so fortunate that Miss Bishop and Mrs. Irvine finished my new dress. Now I'll have someplace to wear it.

11. I Visit Galena and St. Louis with Miss Bishop

Friday, May 19, 1848

I got a ride across the river so I could board the steamer with Miss Bishop. I was welcomed to Kaposia by Dr. Williamson, his wife, and his sister Jane. Miss Bishop looked rested. I told her how pleased and excited I was to get her note. The Williamsons, all three, are among the kindest people I have ever met. Jane Williamson showed me her school for Dakota children. The school is in a fine building. It is well supplied with nice benches for the children. I hope the one built in St. Paul this summer will be just as good. We also strolled through the village, stopped at several bark lodges, and played with the children. I noticed curiosity in the children's faces when they met me. Maybe it is because I am a Métis girl all dressed up to go to St. Louis.

Monday, May 22, 1848

Before we boarded the steamboat, Chief Little Crow himself came by to greet Miss Bishop, and he shook hands with me, too. Two stewards took our bags and led us along the deck to a little room with two beds. It was not a stylish room, but it was practical, with a place for us to hang clothes, a table, and two chairs.

After we were settled in our room, we went up on deck, where Miss Bishop rested on a deck chair with a footrest. She stayed there for several hours because she thinks the sun will help her get her strength back. She also told me that one reason she is taking this trip is to give the Irvine family more time to mourn for Viola in private. She is still grieving for that precious little girl herself.

I leaned against the boat rails as we glided past green bushes and willows, which swept down to the shore. It was a peaceful scene and a welcome change from bumping along on a creaky Red River cart.

After a while I walked around the steamer. It is fascinating, like a town floating on the river. The stewards were busy working all about the boat. I had never seen people with skin that black before. I wonder where they have come from. They made jokes and teased each other when they thought no one was watching. The passengers call them "darkies."

Miss Bishop says we will stop overnight in Galena, Illinois, to visit Mrs. Jones, with whom she shared a room when she came upriver. They had exchanged addresses because Mrs. Jones was concerned about Miss Bishop going alone to a place with such a rowdy reputation.

After we stay overnight with Mrs. Jones, we'll take the next boat to St. Louis, where we'll stay until we can catch a boat back to St. Paul.

During the long hours on deck Miss Bishop told me all about growing up on a farm near the shore of Lake Champlain with her parents and sisters. She also taught school in New York State and took a ferry across the lake each time she visited her family. She says that coming alone on the journey to Minnesota was the most adventurous experience of her life. Seeing Miss Bishop relaxing in the deck chair is quite a change. Until now she has always seemed to be busy every single moment.

We talked for hours as we glided along on the river. I told her more about my teachers, Mlles Angelique and Marguerite Nolin, and how they had planned to send me to the school they attended in Montreal.

"Don't give up your dreams, Josette," Miss Bishop said. "They're still possible if you keep them in your mind and in your heart." Miss Bishop said that her home in northern Vermont is not far from Montreal, but that she had never been there. Maybe if she goes back to Vermont and I go to Montreal, we could visit each other.

I told her how Mama and the baby died, and she sympathized with the difficult times our family has had.

"You've had to be a mother to your brothers ever since," Miss Bishop said. "I've seen how well you care for Armond. And Pierre was so proud of you that day I needed an interpreter. He knew you'd be able to help me."

Tuesday, May 23, 1848

Miss Bishop asked me to bring her breakfast to the room this morning. We sat by our little window and watched people walk around the boat deck. In the afternoon I got tea for her. I'm glad to do it. I know she asked me to come along to do little things for her.

At mealtime we usually go to the dining room. It has a crystal chandelier that makes the gold trim on the doors sparkle. I was nervous at first and didn't know what to do when the steward pulled out a red velvet chair for me. Miss Bishop told me he was just trying to help me sit down! Did he imagine that I didn't know how? Then I noticed the stewards were helping all the ladies.

Tonight at dinner we could choose between mutton, steak, or cold ham, or we could try all three. Corn bread, baked potatoes, and sliced bananas were arranged on fancy platters. Five kinds of cake were displayed for dessert. The stewards in white uniforms with gold-braid trimming kept offering us food. I'm writing this down so I can tell Armond and Pierre all about the feast when I get home.

Later I watched the stewards hoist buckets of water out of the river to serve as drinking water at the tables. I remember that earlier today as I passed by the kitchen the cooks laughed as they tossed pieces of meat across the room to each other. All the fine food no longer seems so appetizing. We stopped at Prairie du Chien today. That's where the Irvines used to live.

Wednesday, May 24, 1848

Today we stopped near Galena, Illinois. Mrs. Jones met us, and we rode by carriage to her house. She pointed out buildings as we passed between the river landing and the town. This area is becoming well known for lead and zinc mining, Mrs. Jones said.

Dr. and Mrs. Jones's house almost took my breath away. It's a tall brick mansion with a wrought iron fence around it. Mrs. Jones said that it is one of the finest homes in Galena.

Mrs. Jones showed us the rooms on the main floor; then Miss Bishop and I were led upstairs to separate bedrooms. After the door to my bedroom closed, I looked around at the tall headboard, the immense armoire, and the heavy draperies that hung at the windows. I was overwhelmed. I felt guilty in all this luxury and realized I ought to be back home with Papa and the boys.

Soon there was a knock at the door. Miss Bishop slipped in and whispered, "Don't be afraid, Josette. I'm not used to this, either. We'll just pretend we're accustomed to being in a place like this. After I rest awhile, we can go downstairs together."

I breathed a sigh of relief, knowing that Miss Bishop was a little uncomfortable, too. We were invited onto the veranda for tea. Mrs. Jones poured from a pot into china cups so delicate I could almost see through them. I thought of Mama's treasured cups, still stored carefully at our cabin, but surely these were finer. I looked down at my hands holding that dainty handle, then past the wrought iron railing to where the crocuses and daffodils grew. Mama could never have imagined her daughter in a house like this.

After tea we strolled through the garden to see the flower beds of pansies and marigolds. Mrs. Jones suggested that we rest in our rooms for a while and said that dinner was served at seven.

Upstairs in my room I felt so alone. I tried to sit on the edge of the bed; but it was too high, so I sat down in a gliding rocker. I had never slept in a room all by myself before. In St. Eustache our house had three rooms, the main one and two bedrooms, one for Mama and Papa, and one for the children. I was so glad I had the lovely dress Miss Bishop and Mrs. Irvine made for me to wear. I yearned to go back to our room on the boat, which seemed plenty fancy to me.

Miss Bishop knocked for me at seven, and as we

walked down to dinner her heels clattered on the polished wood steps and echoed in the hall. We paused at the dining-room door and saw a table set with tall silver candlesticks. The whole room gleamed from the light of the candles. As Dr. and Mrs. Jones invited us to be seated at the table I stared at the row of silver knives, forks, and spoons at each place. I was grateful that Miss Bishop had warned me to wait to see which fork or spoon Mrs. Jones used before I picked up any of them.

Mrs. Jones rang a little bell for the maid, Eliza, to come in.

"I'm surprised that you stayed in St. Paul to open a school," Mrs. Jones said to Miss Bishop at dinner. "When I visited there, it was a squalid little river town." Miss Bishop sat up straight at that remark and defended the growing village.

"Minnesota is a beautiful place, and I have come to love the people there," Miss Bishop replied, and then added, "They needed a school desperately. I want to bring the advantages of learning and culture to its citizens."

At dinner I sat in fear of doing something wrong. There were no mishaps that I know of.

Mrs. Jones chatted about this and that, then paused

when she looked at me and asked, "Are most of the people living in St. Paul half-breeds like this girl?"

Miss Bishop turned to me and said in a calm, friendly voice, "Josette, would you speak to Mrs. Jones in French and tell her, 'Thank you so much for the fine dinner and warm hospitality'?"

I think she wanted Mrs. Jones to know that I wasn't as ignorant and uneducated as she had assumed.

"Madame, merci pour un repas formidable et aussi pour nous acquérir chaleureusement," I said.

After dinner Dr. Jones excused himself to go to the library to smoke. Mrs. Jones and Miss Bishop went into the parlor to talk. I was relieved when Mrs. Jones said I could go into the kitchen and talk to Eliza. I think Mrs. Jones wanted to be alone with Miss Bishop to ask her more questions about life in St. Paul.

Although Eliza had shiny black skin like the men on the ship, the palms of her hands and her fingernails were pink. I wondered if the black had worn off because of the hard work she did. Eliza's white teeth filled her smile when she said no. She showed me every corner of the kitchen and opened the pantry cupboards where all the fine dishes were stored. She has never been to school, she said, and can't write her name.

While we were talking, Eliza washed the fine china plates with gold rims and I dried them. As we were working, one of the plates slipped when we passed it between us. It slipped from our hands and fell to the floor in a crash. Eliza's hands started to tremble. I was afraid, too. Mrs. Jones came to the kitchen door with an angry look. I was sure she was going to punish Eliza.

"Mrs. Jones, one of your best plates slipped out of my hands and fell to the floor," I said. "I'm very sorry. It wasn't Eliza's fault. How can I ever replace it?" Eliza was quickly sweeping up the pieces. Mrs. Jones had a harsh look on her face, but she turned it to a set smile and said that I should not feel responsible for it.

After Mrs. Jones left, I asked Eliza why she was so afraid. Eliza said that her last master would have whipped her for breaking a dish. She had me feel the scars on her back. She said this was a very nice house to live in, and she hoped that she could always have Dr. Jones for a master. She said the worst thing that could happen to her would be if she was put up for sale at a slave auction. Anyone living farther south in a slave state could buy her then.

I stayed with Eliza until Mrs. Jones came and told me that Miss Bishop was ready to go to her room. As I walked up the polished wood stairway I thought about the hard life a slave must have. I wished I could have seen the room where Eliza slept. Was it in the house, or in a little place back beyond the flower gardens? I lay awake a long time, thinking about Eliza and the worries she had. I felt very grateful for the life I have.

When I get back home, I will tell Lillie and Emilie all about this trip, the good parts and also the bad. I wonder if Amanda has ever seen a slave or a house this grand.

The next morning after breakfast, we took the carriage to board the boat for St. Louis. I was relieved to be leaving. I told Miss Bishop about the plate, and she apologized to Mrs. Jones, too. After we were on our way, she said that accidents happen to everyone, so I shouldn't let it spoil the rest of our journey.

Thursday, May 25, 1848

We passed by Muscatine, Iowa, this evening, and the captain announced that we would go by Burlington, Iowa, at one in the morning. While in bed I felt the boat stop and went up on deck to look. As the moon shone on the water, boxes and barrels were loaded and unloaded. Thankfully, Miss Bishop seemed to be asleep.

Friday, May 26, 1848

This morning the weather turned cold. It was so windy and rainy that the boat docked in Keokuk for the whole day. Miss Bishop began to regret her decision to go on to St. Louis. While we were docked, Miss Bishop and I had several hours to talk.

One of the things she told me is that girls should not marry too young. I should get to know several young men, she said, but wait until I'm older to promise myself to one. I asked her what she thought of Denis, and she agreed that he was one of the nicest young men she has met. She did hint that it might be best to marry someone with as much education, if not more, than I will have when I finish school. Denis is older than I am. Many girls would like to know him better and perhaps marry him. I don't want to give up my dream of going to Montreal. Miss Bishop said she knows of several places where I could get teacher's training in the United States. That gave me a little peace of mind.

Miss Bishop told me she has had many disappoint-ments in her life, when things didn't go the way she thought they should. I should expect that I will have disappointments in the future, she said, because they are part of life. It seems to me that one reason Miss Bishop asked me along must be because she doesn't like to travel alone, even though she came all alone to St. Paul last year. We've spent a lot of time talking on this trip. I learned she is going to be thirty-one on her next birthday.

Miss Bishop said she feels fully recovered from the pneumonia, but she still gives me little errands to do.

Saturday, May 27, 1848

When we arrived in St. Louis today, the levee was bustling, and we were happy to leave it once our luggage was brought off the boat. We took a carriage to a hotel Mrs. Jones had recommended. The lobby of the hotel had high ceilings and velvet draperies at the tall windows. Gaslights in fancy sconces hung on the walls. Our room has a high ceiling, a high bed with velvet draperies hanging around the headboard, and a tall armoire. At least our clothes took up very little space. This hotel is even grander than Dr. and Mrs. Jones's house!

The proprietor of the hotel warned us that there was cholera in St. Louis this spring and so we must drink only water that has been boiled.

"All the water at the hotel is safe to drink," the proprietor said, "but be careful about eating anywhere but the hotel dining room."

Miss Bishop was skeptical. We saw people were eating in many restaurants. She thinks he wants us to spend our money at his hotel. He warned us about the park also.

"You ladies might wish to take a stroll through Lafayette Park, but keep to the outer edges because the inner part is still a muddy wilderness. It is a park set aside just last year," he said.

Today we went to look at the buildings. Most buildings here have brick and stone decorations. We found the Mercantile Library and saw hundreds of books on its shelves. I learned that St. Louis started as a fur-trade center and that the early settlers were French, just like many places in Canada. The immigrants who arrived later spoke German, and we heard *Wie geht est Ihnen?* and *Guten Tag* as we were walking on the street. German sounds quite different from French.

It was getting dark when we returned to the hotel. The streets were lined with new gaslights set on high pedestals of black wrought iron. They are beautiful! People parade down the sidewalks in the evening just as though it was day. The twinkling lights above their heads make St. Louis look like a fairyland.

Before going into the hotel, we noticed a sign advertising a telegraph.

"A telegraph station right here in St. Louis," Miss Bishop exclaimed. We watched the operator translate the letters into the rapid tap-tap-tap of the coded messages.

"When a relative has news from back East, we don't get the message until months later," Miss Bishop said. "I hope St. Paul gets a telegraph someday." As we watched for a few minutes in the bare little office Miss Bishop decided she must send a message. She asked the telegraph operator to send a message to her sister, Almyra: "On trip to St. Louis. New telegraph office here. Hope you are feeling better. Greetings and love, Harriet." It took most of the money Miss Bishop had with her to pay for the telegram. I felt then that it must have been very hard for Miss Bishop this last year with no mail from family or friends for months at a time.

As we went into the hotel a newsboy held up a paper that announced that St. Louis would soon build the Ohio and Mississippi Railway. It will be possible to come from the East by railcar when it is finished.

Miss Bishop said she is glad I could see the wonders of

progress in St. Louis. It has been exciting to see all the new inventions in St. Louis, but I don't think I'd like to live there.

Monday, June 5, 1848

On the way back I wrote letters to all my friends in Red River. I wrote pages and pages to White Cloud because she may never be able to come here. I told her many tiny details that I think she would want to know. I also told her a little bit about Denis. When we get home to St. Paul, I hope I can find someone to deliver the letters up the trail.

12. We Return to a
New Home and a New School

Thursday, June 8, 1848

We returned to St. Paul in a rainstorm. When we got off the boat at Jackson's Landing, the stewards carried our bags off the boat. I planned to carry Miss Bishop's suitcase for her, but Denis had heard the steamboat whistle and picked us up with a horse and a brand-new wagon.

"Did Mr. Irvine get a new wagon?" I asked. Denis just smiled. When we got to the Irvines' house, Miss Bishop got off, and Denis carried her bag to the door. I thanked her and said that I will never forget the wonderful trip that I had to St. Louis.

By the time we left the Irvines' house, it had stopped raining. As Denis drove, he suddenly stopped the horse under the tamarack trees.

"I want you to get down and walk all around the wagon and have a good look," he said. He wanted me to admire the wagon's gold trim from every angle. He pointed out the fancy sunshade. I told him it was beautiful and the Irvines must be proud to own it.

Then he said, "It's mine. I saved enough working for John Irvine to buy it. I'm going to start a service for people who need rides."

"People will be happy to pay for rides in this shiny new wagon," I said. I wasn't sure what to do next as we were standing together by the side of the wagon, so I hoisted my skirt to climb up into the seat. Just then he put his hands on my shoulders, looked at me, and solemnly kissed me.

"I've been thinking about doing that the whole time you've been gone," he said with a wide smile, the same smile that I remember from that first night of dancing at the buffalo hunt. I was surprised and thrilled. We rode home, sitting side by side, and I felt my heart racing in my chest the whole way. Pierre and Armond came running down the hill when they saw us coming, excited about Denis's new wagon. Papa said they got along fine while I was gone, but I felt very glad to be back home.

Sunday, June 18, 1848

It's been ten days since I last wrote. Many exciting things have been happening. People stop me on the street to ask me about the trip to St. Louis. Denis comes by most every day after he's through giving people rides and working for John Irvine. He's been working on the new schoolhouse, too. Sometimes he practices reading aloud to me. He's decided it is better to learn to read English than French.

Monday, June 26, 1848

Papa is busy with lots of building jobs. Daniel Hopkins's daughter, Elvira, and her husband, Abram Cavender, moved here with their children, Sarah and Charles, to start a wagon-making and blacksmith business that I hope will not hurt Papa's work as a harness maker. Denis heard Mr. Irvine say that the population in St. Paul is going to boom as soon as Minnesota is declared a territory of the United States.

Monday, July 3, 1848

Miss Bishop came back feeling full of energy. She is enthusiastic about turning this place into a real town.

"We are going to have an Independence Day celebration with a band made up of townspeople," she said. She taught the schoolchildren to sing, "My country, tis of thee, Sweet land of liberty, of thee I sing."

The children are making drums out of boxes for a parade. Miss Bishop told us a story about her neighbors in Vermont, whose fathers fought for independence from the British about seventy years ago.

"We should never forget their sacrifice for our liberty," she said. I had already learned from the Nolin sisters that in 1759 the British defeated the French in Quebec City. I don't mind that the British lost the war for American independence. The French lost the most in the end.

Wednesday, July 5, 1848

Miss Bishop has organized a temperance society that asks young men to pledge that they will not drink alcohol. That includes whiskey and rum. Not many

French Canadians are taking the pledge. I have seen Denis drink a little, too, but never enough to get drunk.

James Boal, an artist who just moved here, drew a beautiful certificate with fancy scrolls around the letters to be presented to those who sign the pledge.

The parade for Independence Day was not as grand as Miss Bishop had hoped. There are not enough people living in this town who have patriotic pride, she thinks. All the schoolchildren paraded from the school to the boat landing, but there was only a small band with fiddlers, drummers, and two trumpets. Still, most of the people in town came out to see the parade. When we stopped at the landing, we listened to a short speech by Alex McLeod, leader of the new temperance society. Miss Bishop led the group in singing "America." A steamboat had docked, and the passengers and hands came on deck to watch and clap.

Miss Bishop said she couldn't help but compare the parade with ones she had seen in Vermont and New York, where many people marched in the parade and all the soldiers from the War of Independence and the French and Indian War donned their uniforms and marched, too. Even though this parade was small, Miss Bishop was not discouraged.

Friday, July 14, 1848

Denis gives me a ride whenever there is a dance. Sometimes he tells me that Amanda would like a ride, too. I always say it would be nice if she wants to come, but inside would prefer that she didn't. Even though Miss Bishop likes Denis, she keeps telling me I should know a wider world. She said that since I speak French so well, I should even plan go to Paris someday. Not even the Nolin sisters have been to Paris. When I write to them, I will tell them how very nice our new school is turning out to be.

Miss Bishop has written to the National Board of Popular Education to get another teacher to come to St. Paul. People are moving here so fast that we need two teachers. Miss Bishop says I can stay as her helper, too. She is checking into the closest course for teacher's training, but she says I'm a very good teacher even without more training.

Wisconsin was declared a state earlier this year, but the border ends at the St. Croix River. Some men met near Jackson's Store today to plan a territorial government.

Tuesday, August 1, 1848

Miss Bishop and I have moved all the supplies to the new school building. A desk for the teacher and benches for the students are being built. We will be ready to start in two weeks. I no longer worry about the boys learning to read and do numbers. They'll do all right in this town now that there is a real school. I still miss the Nolin sisters, but Miss Bishop is a very good teacher, too, and can also teach us English. The school will be just as good as the one at Chief Little Crow's village.

Our own cabin is nice, even though the stove has not arrived yet. Denis put up a shelf for Mama's teapot and dainty cups, if I can ever get them from St. Eustache. How I wish Mama could be here with us. She would have loved the new cabin Papa built. We have started a new life in a new town, whether I like it or not. Lillie and Emilie Desmarias and Amanda Irvine are my friends here. And Denis. It is a lot of fun to have a suitor, if that is what he is. He is determined to learn to read and write in English, but it is harder because he didn't learn it as a child.

People stop Papa on the street because they have work for him. There is a widow lady who keeps asking him to come over and fix things at her cabin. I don't know if Papa notices how friendly she is to him, but he always goes to help her.

Miss Bishop keeps writing notes just like I do. She is going to write a book about her early days in St. Paul. She thinks that someday St. Paul will be as big and busy as St. Louis, but she wants to write about the way it was when she found it. Otherwise, no one will ever believe her. Miss Bishop has a suitor now named Mr. James Humphrey. Many people talk about it because he is eight years younger than she. She seems more carefree and much happier. His sister moved here not long ago, and she does not approve because of the age difference. I wonder why it matters so much.

Friday, August 4, 1848

It has been two years to the day since we left St. Eustache, and today I am fifteen. How my life has changed in that time! I think I have changed, too. Even if we were back at St. Eustache, Mama would not be there. I still miss my dear friend White Cloud, my wonderful teachers, and Nokomis as well as Papa's relatives in St. Boniface. But I have had many experiences that I would never have had in St. Eustache. I do want to go back up there someday, but not by oxcart.

There is much to look forward to in this busy town. Buildings are going up in St. Paul as fast as they can be built. Every day Papa and Denis have more work than they can finish. So many French families have come here from Canada that we are never lonely.

Miss Bishop is giving me lessons so I can study beyond the classes she teaches in the school. Someday she hopes to start an academy for students who have finished the elementary grades, like the academy where she used to teach at in Moriah, New York.

I want to get teacher training, although many teachers have never had it. That's my dream, and I won't let go of it. I can't leave my brothers yet.

My feelings are divided. I know it's still my job to take care of the boys until they are a little older, but I do hope to be a teacher. Miss Bishop has written letters back East asking for additional new teachers: one to help her, and one to come to Stillwater. Next year we will need more teachers here, she says, and perhaps as soon as I am sixteen, I can teach officially.

When we left the Red River, I felt the good times were over. We were leaving behind everything that had been Mama's, my teachers, my friends, and all that was familiar. Now I know that the good times are only beginning. We have a new cabin and new friends; and Miss Bishop will help me continue my schooling. I have a wonderful friend in Denis. I am happy all the time. Someday I will go back to the Red River for a visit; and someday I am determined to go to Montreal for a visit, or maybe to study.

On the boat Miss Bishop had said, "Don't give up your dreams, Josette. They're still possible if you keep them in your mind and in your heart."

Afterword

After her arrival in 1847, Harriet Bishop taught school for a time and continued to live in St. Paul. She wrote a book, *Floral Home, or, First Years of Minnesota,* about her early days in the area, where mention is made of "a large half-breed girl who helped translate." Most of the incidents Josette relates after the teacher arrives are mentioned in *Floral Home,* including the arrival of the Red River carts in August 1847, living with the Irvine family, and the tragic death of little Viola Irvine. Miss Bishop did close the school briefly and traveled to Galena after that event, but did not mention a companion.

Harriet Bishop did not marry the suitor she met in 1848. Later she married John McConkey, a widower with several children. When he returned from the American Civil War, they were divorced; and a special act of the state legislature restored her maiden name. Harriet Bishop was active in the passage of the Eighteenth Amendment to the U.S. Constitution, which prohibited the sale of alcoholic beverages, and was an organizer in the fight to secure the vote for women. She also wrote poetry and published a book about the 1862 Dakota Conflict. She traveled to both East and West coasts but made St. Paul her home until her death in 1883.

Angelique and Marguerite Nolin began a school at St. Eustache in 1829 that operated for at least twenty years. The teachers assisted Father Georges Belcourt and others in learning languages and communicating with Native Americans.

Pig's Eye Parrant was a former voyageur who sold whiskey to the soldiers at Fort Snelling until he was banned from the area and moved downstream to St. Paul.

Norman Kittson was a former voyageur who operated Red River cart trains during the 1840s. The cart trains continued for the next thirty years. Kittson served four terms in the Minnesota legislature and in 1858 became the mayor of St. Paul.

The city grew enormously after Minnesota was declared a state in 1858. Many immigrants came down the Red River Trail to make their home in the new state of Minnesota in the years that followed. The Métis, who were the largest group of early settlers, dispersed socially and regionally. Many people living in the Upper Midwest today are their descendants. In the United States most have become a blended part of American society.

Glossary

MÉTIS (MAY-tee) A French word meaning "mixed blood," usually designating persons with a mixed French and Indian heritage. Many Métis living in Canada identify themselves as a separate tribal group.

OJIBWE (o-jib-wa) also spelled Ojibwa or Ojibway. One tribe of a large Algonquin group that migrated from the eastern states, pushed by advancing white settlement. In many treaties negotiated with the U.S. government, they are known as Chippewa. Anishinabe (a-nish-in-a-bay), meaning "first people," is the name many Ojibwe prefer.

Ojibwe people traditionally moved with the seasons. In fall they traveled to wetlands to harvest wild rice. During the winter they lived in the woods, where they could hunt and trap. In spring they tapped maple trees for sap, which they boiled down to make maple syrup and sugar. During the summer they tended gardens of maize and squash.

WILD RICE A grain that grows naturally as tall grass in the shallow shorelines of northern lakes. Called *manomin* (maun-o-min) by the Ojibwe, it is their basic food. When the fur traders encountered it, they called the grain *folle avoine* because it resembled oats. Literally the French words mean "crazy oats."

SELECTED OJIBWE WORDS

anibiminagaawanzh
   (ani-bim-na-gaa-wanzh)   cranberries
bine (bin-ea)   partridge
boozhoo (boo-SHOE)   greeting evolved from the
   French bonjour

daga (dah-gah)   please
innaatig (in-naa-tig)   maple sugar
manomin (maun-o-min)   wild rice
migwetch (mee-gwetch)   thank you
minan (min-nan)   blueberries
nokomis (no-KOH-mis)   grandmother
ogema (oh-geh-ma)   queen
pemmican (pem-mi-can)   dried meat: buffalo, beef,
   or deer (beef jerky is similar)

waawaashkeshi
   (waawaa-sh-keshi)   deer/venison
wigwam (WIHG-wahm)   a birch-bark house

SELECTED DAKOTA WORDS

aunyeyapi (AUN-ye-ye-a-pi)	blueberries
htani (hta-NI)	work
mazahan bosdoka (MAZ-ahan bos-DOKA)	shoot off a gun?
ptehasina (PTENA-hin-sma)	buffalo robe
tatanka (ta-TAN-ka)	buffalo
tatanka wanase (ta-TAN-ka wan-A-see)	buffalo hunt
wanyaka waseaun (wan-YAKA was-SEUN)	seen white man?

SELECTED FRENCH WORDS

adieu (a-DEU)	good-bye
au revoir (ow RUVWAR)	see you soon
billet doux (billy doo)	love letter
bonjour (bon-ZUR)	good morning
brioche (bree-owsh)	a rich, sweet bread
en masse (an MAS)	all together
fiancée (fee-AN-sey)	woman engaged to be married
folle avoine (fall auv-WAUN)	"crazy oats," wild rice

grande dame (graund
   dahm)   venerable woman
pardon (par-DUN)   excuse me
rendezvous (ron-day-VOU) in the fur trade, meetings
                      between voyageurs to
                      exchange goods

DATE DUE

GAYLORD   PRINTED IN U.S.A.